PROBLEM SOLVING AND PYTHON PROGRAMMING

Dr. P. Arockia Mary
Associate Professor
Department of Information Technology
V.S.B. Engineering College, Karur, Tamil Nadu

SHANLAX
#SINCE1990
SHANLAX PUBLICATIONS

PROBLEM SOLVING AND PYTHON PROGRAMMING

First Edition: **2020**

ISBN: 978-93-90082-60-5

"Comments on this book are invited at : arockiamary2001@gmail.com"

Publisher

SHANLAX PUBLICATIONS
61, 66 T.P.K. Main Road
Vasantha Nagar
Madurai – 625003
Tamil Nadu, India

Ph: 0452-4208765,
Mobile: 7639303383
email:publisher@shanlaxpublications.com
web: www.shanlaxpublications.com

FOREWORD

Released in 1990 Python Programming has become the most popular language for its role in Artificial Intelligence (AI) applications, Data Science, Machine Learning (ML) and Data Analytics. Students learn Python in colleges in the entry year itself and become quickly skilled in programming. Python is easy for beginners in programming and students soon enjoy its flexibility and versatility.

A Coursera report says that "Python's open source nature makes it easy to learn. A large number of libraries for tasks like web development, text processing, and calculations adds to its appeal". Python has become an important tool in Data Science. In fact, Python's rapid growth over the past five years has been fuelled by a large and expanding community of data science professionals.

Many books, by Indian as well as by foreign authors, are available in the market for someone desirous of acquiring skills in Python. Books for novice learners undertaking a course in an educational environment are few to come by. It appears there is a need for a beginner's book on Python Programming by a teacher of long experience. This book titled "PROBLEM SOLVING AND PYTHON PROGRAMMING" fulfils that need.

The author of this book has about two decades of experience in collegiate teaching and is a skilled programmer herself. She has a fine reputation as an effective teacher among her students. The author's teaching expertise is evident in this book in presenting the subject in simple and clear language and supporting every concept or topic with numerous examples. Students will find this book easy to read and understand and will find learning Python an enjoyable experience.

While the content of this book caters mainly to Anna University syllabus, the book amply covers the syllabi of various universities on the subject. Beginners of Python will certainly have an enjoyable study with this book and in the end will leave well-motivated for advanced learning.

August 2020

Dr. M. Radhakrishnan
Former Principal & IT Director
Sudharsan Engineering College, Pudukkottai

CONTENTS

UNIT I
ALGORITHMIC PROBLEM SOLVING

Contents

Algorithms, building blocks of algorithms (statements, state, control flow, functions), notation (pseudo code, flow chart, programming language), algorithmic problem solving, simple strategies for developing algorithms (iteration, recursion). Illustrative problems: find minimum in a list, insert a card in a list of sorted cards, guess an integer number in a range, Towers of Hanoi.

1.1 ALGORITHMS

Algorithm is an ordered sequence of finite, well-defined, unambiguous instructions to solve a given problem and produce a desired result for given input in a finite amount of time.

It is a step-by-step procedure for solving a problem.

For accomplishing a particular task, different algorithms can be written. The different algorithms differ in their requirements of time and space. The programmer selects the best suited algorithm for the given task to be solved.

1.1.1 Characteristics of an Algorithm

1. Well-ordered - The steps are in a correct order.
2. Unambiguous - The operation must be clear and it should be understood by computing agent without any further clarification.
3. Effectively computable - An algorithm should be effective. The computing agent can actually carry out the operation.
4. Input - An algorithm should have one or more well-defined inputs.
5. Output - An algorithm should have one or more well-defined outputs.
6. Finiteness - An algorithm should accomplish its tasks in a finite amount of time.

1.1.2 Method for Developing an Algorithm

1. **Define the problem:** The problem statement should be clear and concise.
2. **List the inputs** that are needed to solve the problem and the outputs that the algorithm will produce as a result.
3. **Describe the steps** that are needed to convert or manipulate the inputs to produce the outputs. Start at a high level first, and keep refining the steps until they are effectively computable operations.
4. **Test the algorithm:** choose data sets and verify that the algorithm works.

1.2 BUILDING BLOCKS OF AN ALGORITHM

1.2.1 Statements

A **statement** is a command given to the computer to take a specific action such as: collect the input, process the input and display the output to the screen.

A computer program is a series of statements.

1.2.2 State

State is a transition from one process to another process under specified condition within a time.

1.2.3 Control Structures

A **control structure** specifies the statements to be executed and the order of execution of statements.

1. Sequence

Instructions are executed in sequential order.

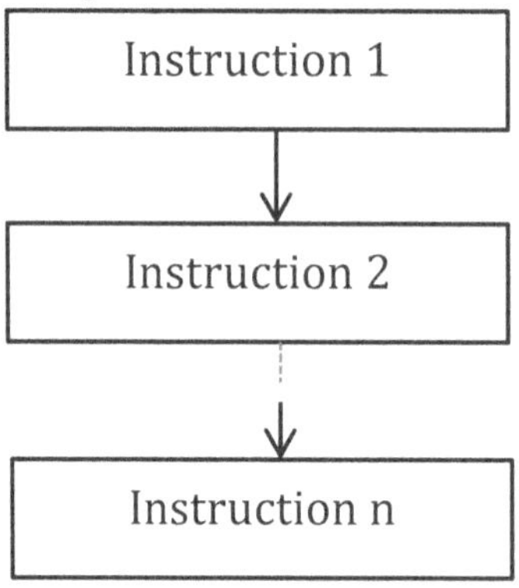

Fig. 1.1

2. Selection /Branching/Conditional

Based on the condition the control is transferred to either True block or False block.

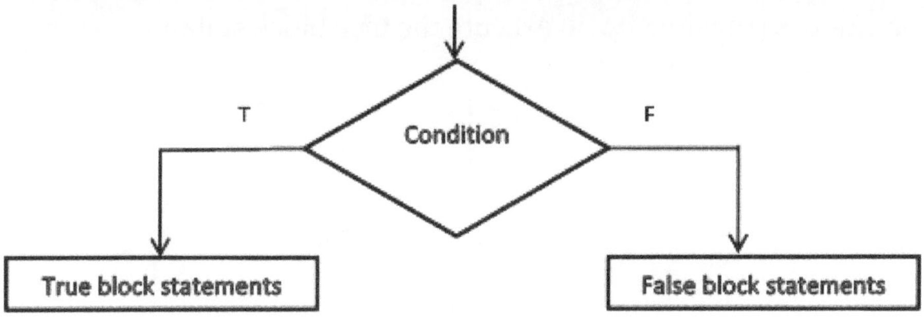

Fig. 1.2

There are different types of selection:

a. **If statement**

Syntax:

```
if (condition)
{
    block of statements
}
```

If the condition is true then it will execute the block of statements otherwise not.

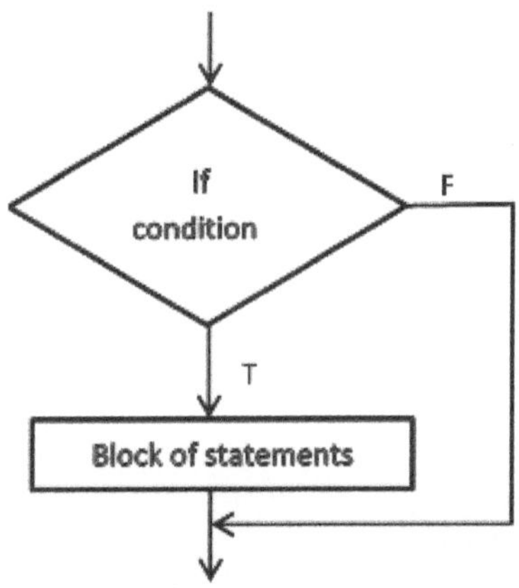

Fig. 1.3

b. **If-Else statement**

Syntax:

```
if (condition)
{
    true block statements
}
Else
{
    false block statements
}
```

If the condition is true then it will execute the true block statements otherwise it will execute false block statements.

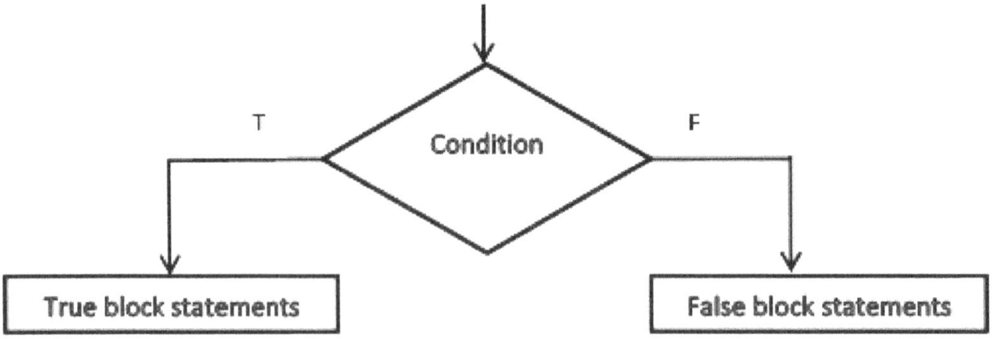

Fig. 1.4

c. If...else if...else statement

Syntax:

```
if (condition 1)
        statements
else if (condition 2)
        statements
.
.
.
else if (condition n)
        statements
else
        statements
```

A user can decide among multiple options and the conditions are executed from the top down. If anyone of *if* conditions is true then the corresponding statements are executed. And the rest of the else-if ladder is bypassed. If none of the conditions are true, then the final *else* statement will be executed.

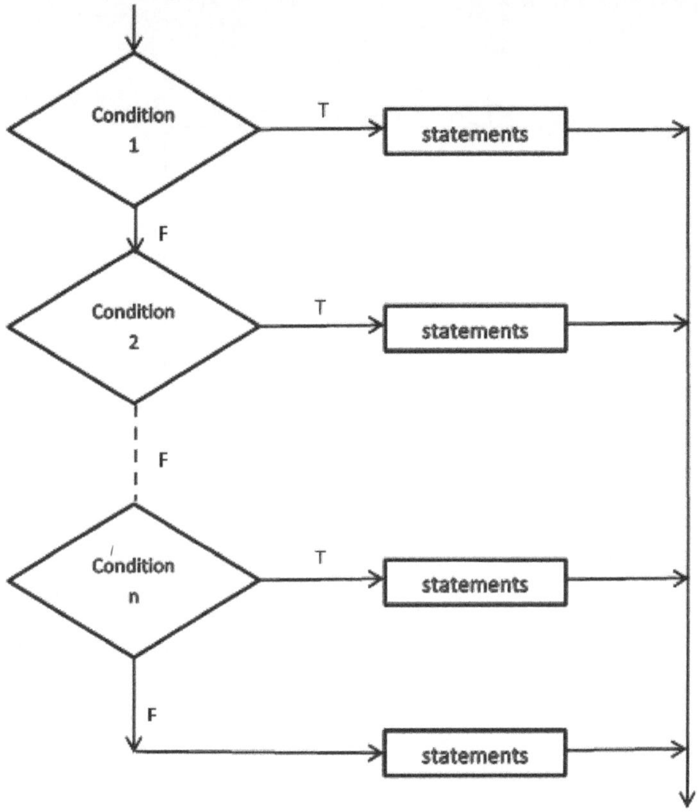

Fig. 1.5

3. Iteration/Looping

It repeats the execution of a block of instructions until the condition is satisfied. There are two types of looping.

a. Entry controlled loop

While loop or For loop

Syntax:

```
while(condition)                for variable=start value to end value
{                               {
        Statements     (OR)             Statements
}                               }
```

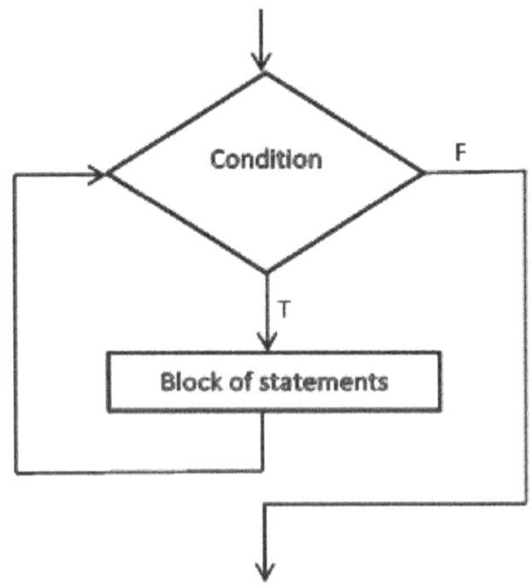

Fig. 1.6

The above diagram shows the entry controlled loop. The *while* condition is used to iterate over a block of statements until the condition is true. In entry controlled loop, the condition is tested initially. If the condition is false then it exits from the loop. The *for* loop executes the statements until the variable reaches the end value.

b. Exit controlled loop

Do-while

Syntax:

```
do
{
        Statements
} while(condition)
```

In exit controlled loop, the condition is tested after the execution of the statements. Even if the condition is false it executes the statements at least once.

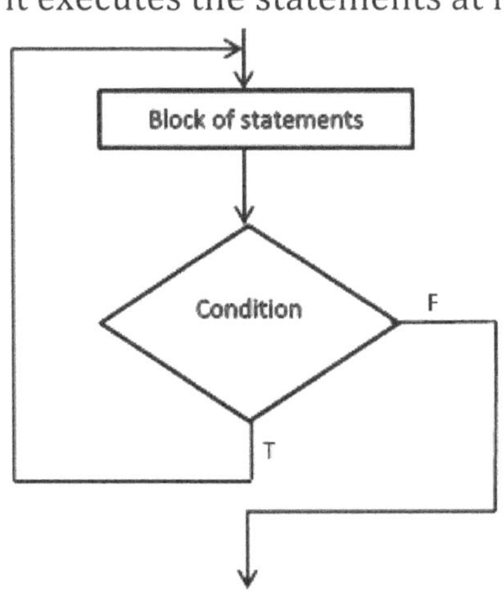

Fig. 1.7

Example 1.1: Write an algorithm to find the biggest/greatest of three numbers.

Step 1: Start

Step 2: Read three numbers X, Y, Z

Step 3: Compare X and Y. If X is bigger then perform step 4 else perform step 5

Step 4: Compare X and Z. If X is bigger then Display "X is the biggest" else Display "Z is the biggest"

Step 5: Compare Y and Z. If Y is bigger then Display "Y is the biggest" else Display "Z is biggest"

Example 1.2: Write an algorithm to check if the given number is Even or Odd

Step 1: Start

Step 2: Read N

Step 3: Check if N is divisible by 2 then go to step 4 else step 5.

Step 4: Display "N is an Even Number" and go to step 6

Step 5: Display "N is an Odd Number"

Step 6: Stop

Example 1.3: Write an algorithm to check if the given year is Leap year or not

Step 1: Start

Step 2: Read year

Step 3: Check if year is divisible by 4 but not 100 then DISPLAY "leap year" and go to step 6

Step 4: Check if year is divisible by 400 then DISPLAY "leap year" and go to step 6

Step 5: Otherwise, DISPLAY "not leap year"

Step 6: Stop

1.2.4 Functions

Function is defined as a subprogram which contains a set of instructions to perform some specific task. Functions provide better modularity for an application and a high degree of code reusing. It is also called as methods, sub-routines and procedure.

A function is often executed several times, from several different places during a single execution of the program. After finishing a subroutine the program will return to the point from where the function is called.

There are two types of functions.

1. User-defined function:

   It is a function which is provided by the user according to their requirement.

2. Built-in function

   It is a predefined function. A function is built into a programming language and can be accessed by end-user.

1.3 NOTATION

Notation is a series or system of written symbols used to represent numbers or some elements. A **notation** can be a pseudo code, flow chart or any programming language.

1.3.1 Pseudocode

- **Pseudocode** consists of short, readable instructions and is formally in English language. It is the outline of program.
- *Pseudo* means imitation or false and *code* means the instruction written in programming language.
- Pseudocode is programming analysis tool that is used for planning program logic.
- It uses plain English statement rather than symbols. It is also known as PEL (Programming English Language).
- Non-programmer also can understand the pseudocode easily.
- Pseudocode cannot be compiled and executed.

Thus, pseudocode is a detailed yet readable description of what a computer program or algorithm must do, expressed in a formally natural language rather than in a programming language.

Rules of pseudocode:

- Use words that are easily translated into computer instructions.
- Use indentation within a loop or a conditional clause.
- Do not include data declarations in pseudo code.

Keywords in pseudocode:

- Some verbs used are **Generate, Compute, Process**, etc.
- Words such as set, reset, increment, compute, calculate, add, sum, multiply, divide, print, display, input, output, edit, test, etc. with careful indentation are used giving desirable pseudocode.

Keywords for use in Pseudocode

Table 1.2

STATEMENTS	KEYWORDS
Input	READ, OBTAIN, GET, INPUT, PROMPT
Output	PRINT, DISPLAY, SHOW
Compute	COMPUTE, CALCULATE, DETERMINE
Initialize	SET, INIT
Add one	INCREMENT
IF, THEN, ELSE, ENDIF	IF-THEN-ELSE
Sequence one	THEN-IF
Sequence two	ELSE-IF
End of IF conditional	ENDIF
WHILE, DO, ENDWHILE	LOOP
CASE, OF, OTHERS, ENDCASE	CASE
Multi-way branch based on conditions	CASE
Identifier before possible CASE conditions	OF
Identifier before CASE default condition, for conditions not listed in the CASE expression	OTHERS
REPEAT,UNTIL loop	REPEAT-UNTIL
REPEAT Sequence	REPEAT
Determine the ending point of a REPEAT Sequence	UNTIL
FOR loop	FOR, TO, DOWNTO, ENDFOR, DO
Iterate with index i from n to m	DOWNTO
Iterate with index i from m to n	TO
FOR Conditional followed by command	FOR
End of FOR loop	ENDFOR
The use of conditional statements inside of other conditional statements	NESTED CONSTRUCTS
Invoking Subprocedures	CALL, RETURN
Addition	ADD
Subtraction	SUB
Multiplication	MUL
Division	DIV

Three basic constructs for flow of control in Pseudocode:

1. Sequence:

- Default mode.
- Each statement in the problem is executed one after another sequentially.

Example 1.4: Pseudo code for adding two numbers

```
READ a, b
COMPUTE sum = a+b
PRINT sum
```

Sample input: 5 4

Ouput: 9

2. Selection:

- A decision making among several conditions/choices. If the condition is True then execute Block1 else Block2
- The basic constructs are
    - i. IF-THEN-ELSE
    - ii. CASE ... ENDCASE

i. If-Then-Else:

- Decision making statement.
- Four key-words: IF, THEN, ELSE, and ENDIF.
- The general form is:

```
IF condition THEN
        Block1
ELSE
        Block2
ENDIF
```

- If the condition is true, Block1 is performed. Otherwise Block2 is performed.

Example 1.5: Pseudo code to check whether the given number is odd or even

```
READ num
IF num MOD 2 = = 0 THEN
        PRINT "Number is Even"
ELSE
        PRINT "Number is Odd"
ENDIF
```

Sample Input: 5

Output: Number is Odd

- **NESTED CONSTRUCTS:** Constructs can be embedded within another construct.
    - **General Form:**

```
IF (condition1) THEN
        IF (condition2) THEN
                Block of Statements
        ENDIF
ENDIF
```

Example 1.6: To find the smallest among three numbers using nested IF construct.

```
READ a, b, c
IF a < b THEN
        IF a < c THEN
                PRINT a
        ELSE
                PRINT c
        ENDIF
ELSE IF b < c THEN
        PRINT b
ELSE
        PRINT c
ENDIF
```

Sample Input: 5 1 8
Output: 1

ii. CASE:

- It is a multiway branch (decision) based on the value of an expression.
- **Four keywords: CASE, OF, OTHERS and ENDCASE.**
- The general form is:

```
CASE expression OF
        condition 1: statements
        condition 2: statements
        ...
        condition n: statements
        OTHERS: default sequence
ENDCASE
```

  - OTHERS clause is optional.
  - Conditions are normally numbers or characters indicating the value of "expression".

Example 1.7: PSEUDO CODE for simple calculator

```
READ m, n, ch
CASE ch OF
        1: PRINT m+n
        2: PRINT m-n
        3: PRINT m*n
        4: PRINT m/n
ENDCASE
```

Sample Input: 5 10 1

Output: 15

3. Iteration / repetition / looping

- One or more instructions are executed repeatedly until the condition is satisfied (true).
- The constructs are:
  i. WHILE ... DO... ENDWHILE
  ii. REPEAT ... UNTIL
  iii. FOR ... ENDFOR

i. WHILE ... DO ... ENDWHILE

While is a loop with a condition at its beginning. The loop is entered only if the condition is true.

General form:

```
WHILE condition DO
        statements
ENDWHILE
```

Example 1.8: PSEUDO CODE to print the numbers from 1 to 5

```
INIT n = 1
WHILE n ≤ 5 DO
        DISPLAY n
        INCREMENT n by 1
ENDWHILE
```

Output: 1 2 3 4 5

ii. REPEAT ... UNTIL

REPEAT...UNTIL loop is similar to the WHILE loop, but the test is performed at the end instead of at the top. The sequence is executed at least once irrespective of the condition.

The general form is:

```
REPEAT
        statements
UNTIL condition
```

Example 1.9: Pseudo code to print the numbers from 1 to 5

```
INIT n=1
REPEAT
        DISPLAY n
        INCREMENT n by 1
UNTIL n ≤ 5
```

Sample Output: 1 2 3 4 5

iii. FOR...ENDFOR

FOR is a "counting" loop. This loop is executed for a specific number of times.

The general form is:

```
FOR iteration bounds
        statements
ENDFOR
```

Example 1.10: To print the numbers from 1 to 5.

```
FOR n = 1 to 5
        PRINT n
ENDFOR
```

Output: 1 2 3 4 5

Control Structures of Pseudocode:

Table 1.3

Sequence	**Selection**	**Iteration**

BEGIN
READ A, B
COMPUTE C=A+B
DISPLAY C
END
	BEGIN
	READ A, B
	IF A>B THEN
	DISPLAY "A is Bigger"
	ELSE
	DISPLAY "B is Bigger"
	ENDIF
	END
		BEGIN
		SET i=1, sum=0
		WHILE i<=5
		COMPUTE
		sum=sum+i
		ENDWHILE
		END

Advantages of Pseudocode:

- Since it is independent of any language, it can be used by most programmers.
- It is easy to develop a program from pseudocode than from a flowchart.
- It is easy to translate pseudocode into a programming language.
- Pseudocode is compact and does not tend to run over many pages.

Disadvantages of Pseudocode

- It does not provide visual representation of the program's logic.
- There are no accepted standards for writing pseudocodes.
- It cannot be compiled nor executed.

1.3.2 Flowchart

Flowchart is a diagrammatic representation of the logic for solving a task. It is drawn using boxes of different shapes with line connecting them to show the flow of control.

Symbols used in Flowchart

Different symbols are used for different states in flowchart.

For example: Input/Output and decision making has different symbols. The table below describes all the symbols that are used in making flowchart

Table 1.4

Symbols	Symbol Name	Description
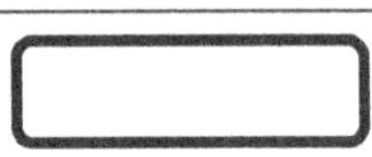	Terminal (Stop/Start)	Used to represent start and end of flowchart
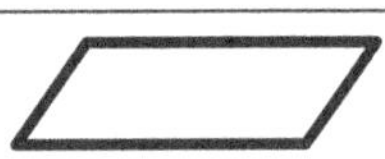	Input / Output	Used for input and output operation.
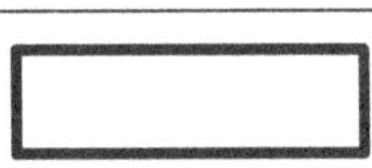	Processing	Used for arithmetic operations and data-manipulations.
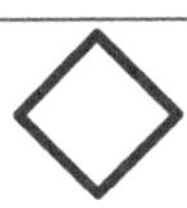	Decision	Used to represent the operation in which there are two alternatives: true and false.
	On-page Connector	Used to join different flow lines
	Off-page Connector	Used to connect flowchart portions on different pages.
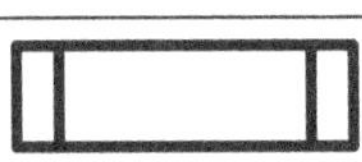	Predefined Process/Function	Used to represent a group of statements performing one processing task.
	Flow line	Used to indicate the flow of logic by connecting symbols.

Guidelines for drawing a flowchart

- The flowchart should be clear, neat and easy to follow.
- The flowchart must have a logical start and finish.
- Only one flow line should come out from a process symbol.

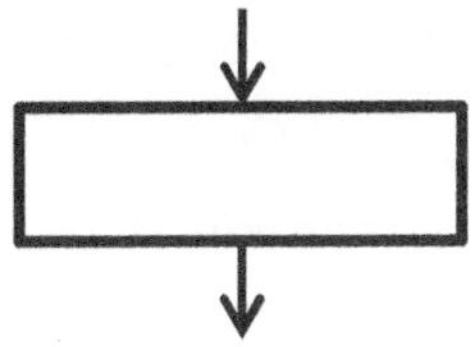

- Only one flow line should enter a decision symbol, but two or three flow lines may leave the decision symbol.

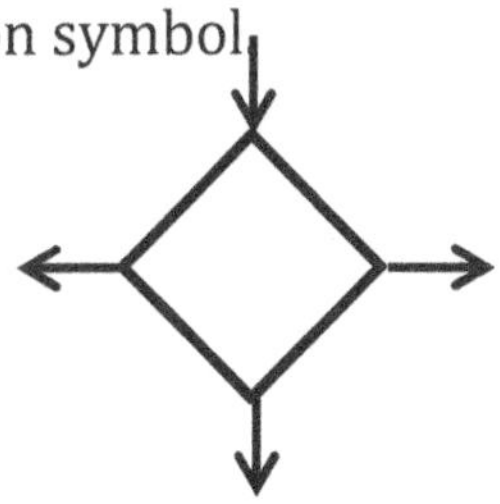

- Only one flow line is used with a terminal symbol.

- Within standard symbols, write briefly and precisely.
- Intersection of flow lines should be avoided.
- If the flowchart becomes complex, it is better to use connector symbols to reduce the number of flow lines.
- It is useful to test the validity of the flowchart by passing through it with a simple test data.

Reasons for using flowcharts as a problem solving tool

Before coding the program the programmer must know about the logic of the program. To make the logic easier to understand the programmer has to study the steps and provide a pictorial representation of the logic. Only if the programmer has clear idea about the logic, he/she will produce a good program. The main reasons for using flowcharts are:

1. **Better Communication** : Flowcharts are better way of communicating the logic of a system.
2. **Effective Analysis** : With the help of flowcharts problem can be analysed in a more effective way.
3. **Proper documentation** : Flowcharts are used for good program documentation which may be needed for various purposes.
4. **Effective coding** : Flowcharts act as a guide or blueprint during the system analysis and program development phase.
5. **Proper debugging** : Flowchart helps in debugging process.
6. **Efficient program maintenance** : The maintenance of program becomes easy with the help of flowchart.

Advantages of flowchart:

- Flowchart helps to clarify how things are currently working and how they could be improved.
- Flowcharts provide graphical representation of actions to be taken.

Limitations of flowchart:

- **Complex Logic:** Sometimes, the program logic is quite complicated. In that case, flowchart becomes complex and clumsy.
- **Alterations and Modifications:** If alterations are required the flowchart may require re-drawing completely.
- **Reproduction:** As the flowchart symbols cannot be typed, reproduction of flowchart becomes a problem.

Rules for drawing the flowchart:

1. Standard symbols should only be used.
2. The arrowheads in the flowchart represent the direction of flow of control.
3. Flow direction is from top to bottom or left to right.
4. Flow lines should not cross each other.

5. Be consistent in using names and variables in the flowchart.
6. Keep the flowchart as simple as possible.
7. Words in the flowchart symbols should be simple and easy to understand.
8. Plan and incorporate all the details of logic related to the problem.
9. If new page is needed, then use connectors.

Control Structures in flowchart:

1. **Sequence**

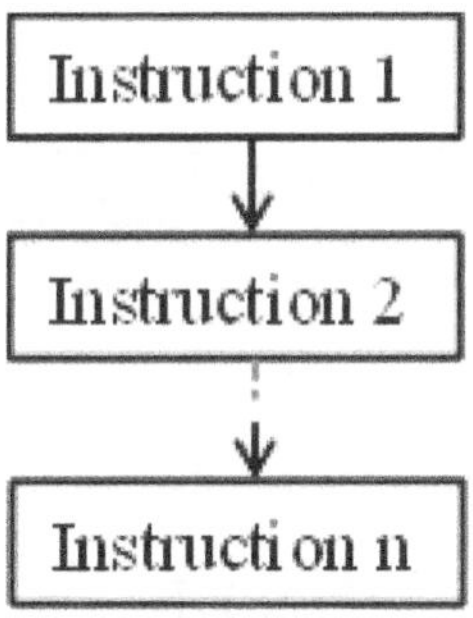

Fig. 1.8

2. **Selection**

   a. **Simple if**

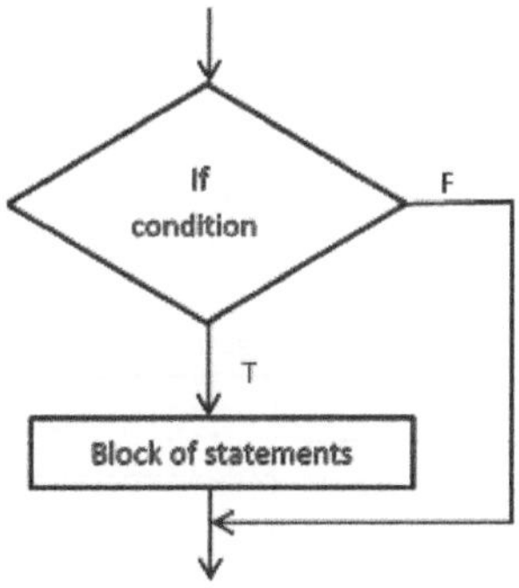

Fig. 1.9

   b. **If-else**

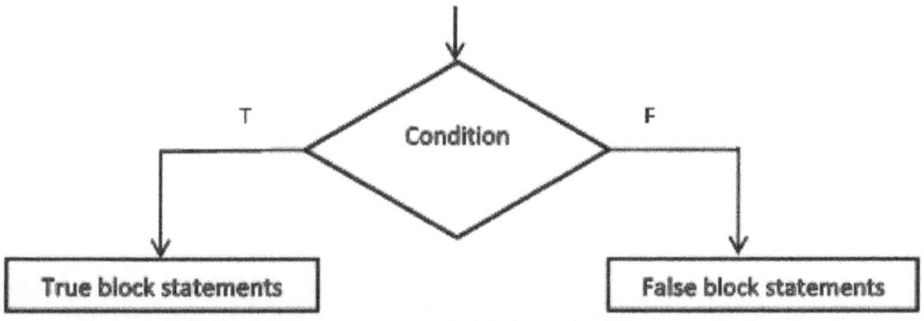

Fig. 1.10

c. If-elseif-else

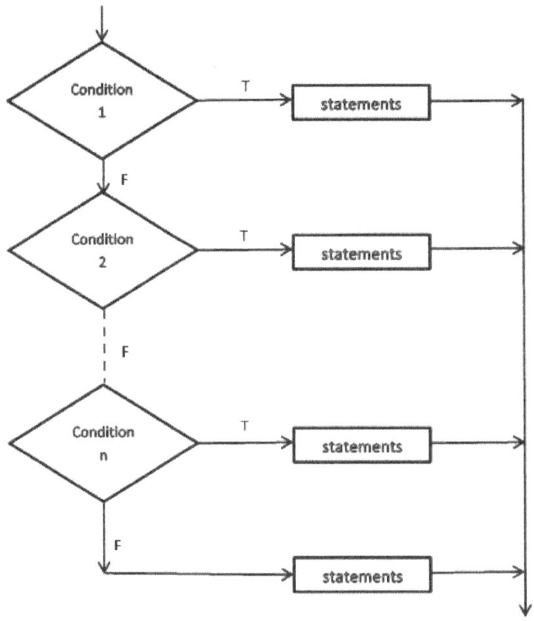

Fig. 1.11

3. Iteration

a. While loop

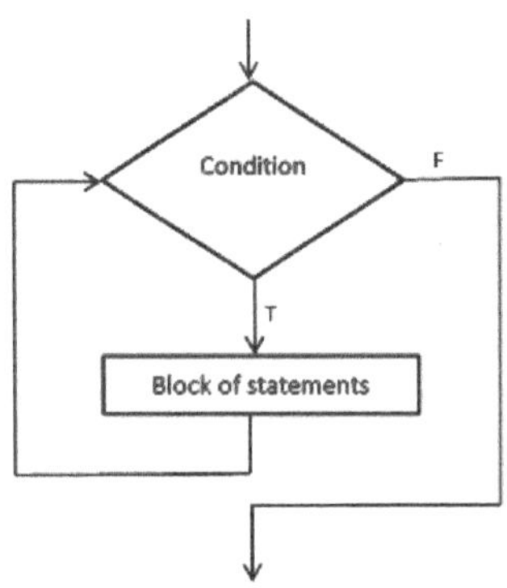

Fig. 1.12

b. Repeat until

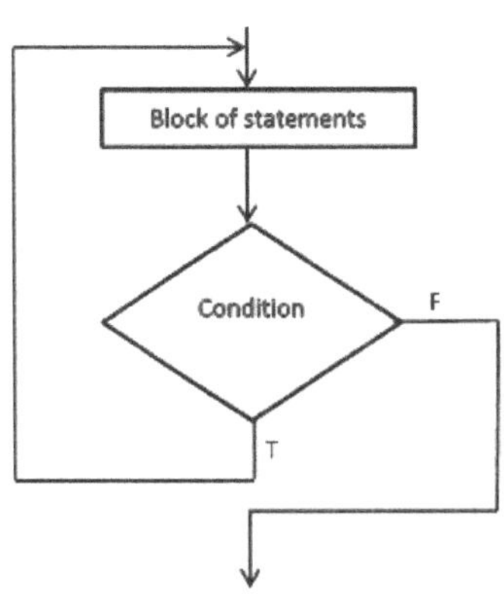

Fig. 1.13

1.3.3 Programming Language

Human languages are known as natural languages. Computers cannot understand natural languages but understand only computer programming language. Programming is the process of translating the algorithm into the syntax of a given programming language.

The steps for writing a computer program are:

1. Understand the problem statement
2. Write an algorithm for that problem
3. Draw the flowchart
4. Write a computer program.
5. Execute the program

Fig. 1.14

Each algorithm step is converted into one or more statements in a programming language.

Program is a sequence of instructions that tells a computer how to do a task.

There are three types of programming language.

i) Low Level Language
ii) Assembly Level Language
iii) High Level Language

i) Low Level / Machine Level Language

Machine language is the only language understood by computers. It is expressed in 0's and 1's. It is very difficult to use for humans.

ii) Assembly Level Language

Assembly language is also a low level programming language. It consists of mnemonic codes instead of 0's and 1's.

The word *low* does not imply that the language is inferior to high level but rather refers to the small amount of abstraction between the language and machine language, because of this low level languages are sometimes described as being "close to the hardware".

Assembly language implements a symbolic representation of the numeric machine codes (MOV, ADD, etc.) and other constants needed to program a particular CPU architecture.

A utility program called an **Assembler** is used to translate assembly language statements (mnemonic statements) into machine code.

iii) High Level Language

High Level Language is a set of words and symbols which a programmer uses to write a program.

High Level Languages are much closer to human language.

Example: BASIC, COBOL, FORTRAN, etc.

High Level Language must use interpreter or compiler translator to convert human understandable program to computer readable code.

Compiler:

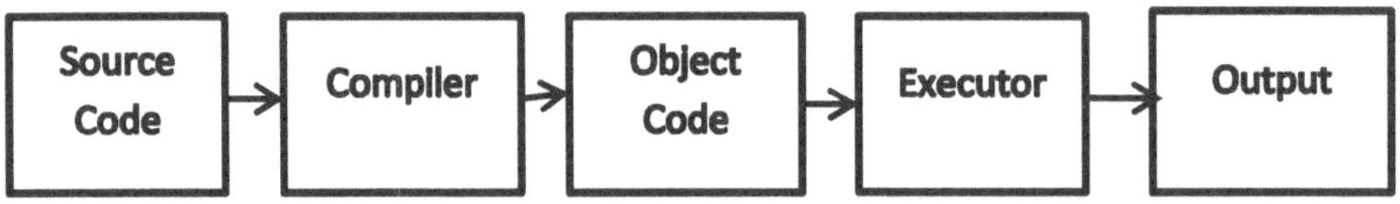

Fig. 1.15

Interpreter:

Fig. 1.16

The differences between an interpreter and a compiler are given below:

Table 1.5

Interpreter	Compiler
Translates a program one statement at a time.	Scans the entire program and translates it as a whole into machine code.
It takes less amount of time to analyse the source code but the overall execution time is slower.	It takes large amount of time to analyse the source code but the overall execution time is comparatively less.
No intermediate object code is generated, hence are memory efficient.	Generates intermediate object code which further requires linking, hence requires more memory.
Continues translating the program until the first error is met, in which case it stops. Hence debugging is easy.	It generates any error message only after scanning the whole program. Hence debugging is comparatively hard.
Programming languages like Python use interpreters.	Programming languages like C, C++ use compilers.

Advantages of High-level language

1. It is like English language, that is, it is easy to read, write and maintain.
2. It makes complex programming simple.
3. It is portable, i.e., it can work on different operating system platforms.
4. Length of the program is also small compared to low-level.
5. Many real time problems can be easily solved with high-level language.

1.4 ALGORITHMIC PROBLEM SOLVING

The problem solving process starts with the problem specification and ends with a correct program.

The steps in the problem solving process are:

1. Problem definition
2. Problem analysis
3. Algorithm development
4. Program coding
5. Program testing and debugging
6. Documentation

1. Problem definition

Define or specify the problem by answering the following questions:

- What the computer program should do?
- What tasks will it perform?
- What kind of data will it use, and where will it get the data?
- What will be the output of the program?
- How will the program interact with the computer user?

Specifying the problem requirements forces the programmer to state the problem clearly.

2. Problem Analysis

It involves identifying the problem parts.

1. Identify the inputs that are needed to solve the problem.
2. Identify the computation to be performed using these inputs.
3. Identify the outputs desired after the computation

3. Algorithm Development

Write an algorithm i.e., step by step procedure to solve the problem.

The development can be expressed as:

a. Pseudocode: Pseudocode describes the outline of a program, written in a form that can easily be converted into computer programming statement.
b. Flowchart: Flowchart is the diagrammatic representation of the algorithm.

4. Program Coding

Program coding is the process of translating the algorithm into the syntax of a given computer programming language. Convert each step in the algorithm into one or more statements in a programming language.

5. Program testing and debugging

Program testing means running the program and executing all its instructions or functions step by step and verify whether it produces the correct result or not.

Debugging is the process of finding and correcting the mistakes in the program code. Errors in the program may be:

Syntax errors – Interpreter or compiler displays an error message. Syntax refers to the grammar of a programming language and rules about the program structure.

Run-time errors – When running a program it may not get executed due to technical errors. This type of error is called Run-time error.

Logical/Semantic errors – The program may run successfully but may not produce the correct result. This may be due to some wrong procedure or wrong usage of keywords or data. Such errors are known as Logical or Semantic errors.

Table 1.6

Testing	Debugging
1. Finding and locating the defect 2. Done by the testing team 3. Intention behind is to find as many defects as possible	1. Fixing the defect 2. Done by the development team 3. Intention is to remove those defects

6. Documentation

Documenting the program is done by the programmer.

Internal Documentation: Internal documentation consists of remarks or comments written with the program instructions to explain what is being done in the program.

External Documentation: External documentation is made up of the manuals or help menus with respect to running the program.

1.5 SIMPLE STRATEGIES FOR DEVELOPING ALGORITHMS

The simple strategies for developing an algorithm are:

a) Iteration b) Recursion

a) Iteration

- Blocks of statements are executed repeatedly until the given condition becomes false.
- Each repetition of the process is also called iteration and the result of the iteration is used as the starting point for the next iteration.

Iterative structures:

There are 3 types of iterative structures.

i) While loop/ Entry-controlled loop/Top-tested loop

While loop is used to iterate over a block statements until the condition is true. In entry-controlled loop, the condition is tested initially. If the condition is false then it exits from the loop.

Syntax:

```
WHILE (condition)
        Statements
ENDWHILE
```

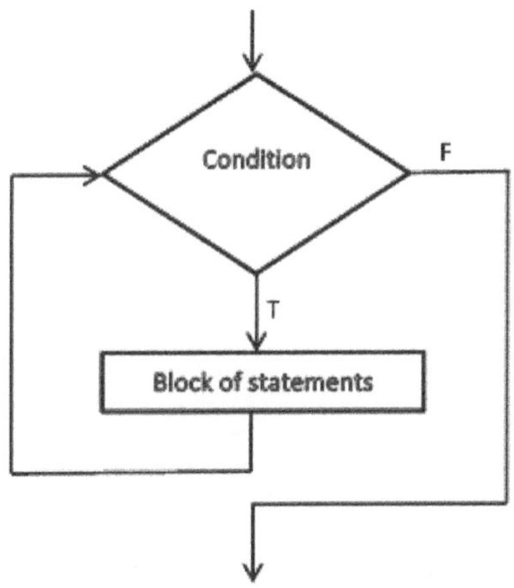

Fig. 1.17

ii) Do-while loop/Exit-controlled loop/Bottom-tested loop

In exit-controlled loop, the condition is tested at last. Even if the condition is false it executes the statements at least once.

Syntax:

```
DO
        Statements
WHILE (condition)
ENDDO
```

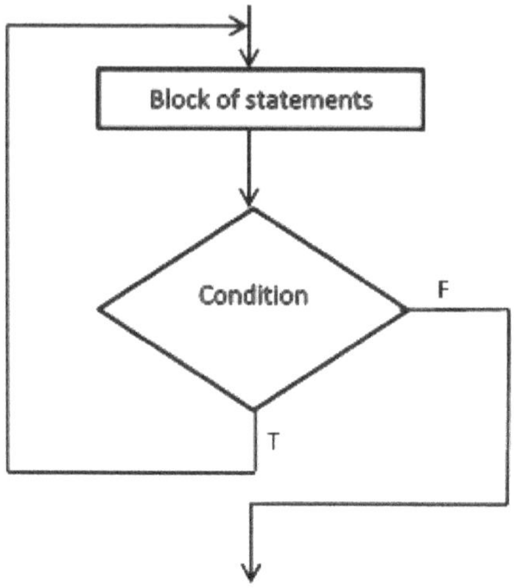

Fig. 1.18

iii) For loop

Block of statements is executed until the given condition becomes false.

Three actions are performed:

1. Initialization
2. Condition
3. Increment/Decrement

Syntax:

```
FOR variable=initial value TO end value
            Statements
ENDFOR
```

Table 1.7

While	Do-while
1. This is top tested loop/entry controlled loop	1. This is bottom tested loop/exit controlled loop
2. The condition is tested initially. If the condition is true then the block of statements is executed until the condition becomes false.	2. It executes the block of statements and then checks the condition. If it is true then block of statements is executed until the condition becomes false.
3. Block of statements will not be executed if the condition is false.	3. Even if the condition is false it executes the block of statements at least once.

Example 1.11: Factorial of a number using while loop

Algorithm:

STEP 1: Start

STEP 2: Read the value of 'n'

STEP 3: Assign the values of i=1 and fact=1

STEP 4: Check whether i<=n using while loop. If the condition is true, then goto step 5 else goto step 6

STEP 5: Calculate fact=fact*i, i=i+1, goto step4

STEP 6: Print fact

STEP 7: Stop

Pseudocode:

```
BEGIN
        READ n
        SET  i=1, fact=1
        WHILE  i<=n
            CALCULATE  fact=fact*i
            INCREMENT  i
        ENDWHILE
        PRINT  fact
END
```

Flowchart

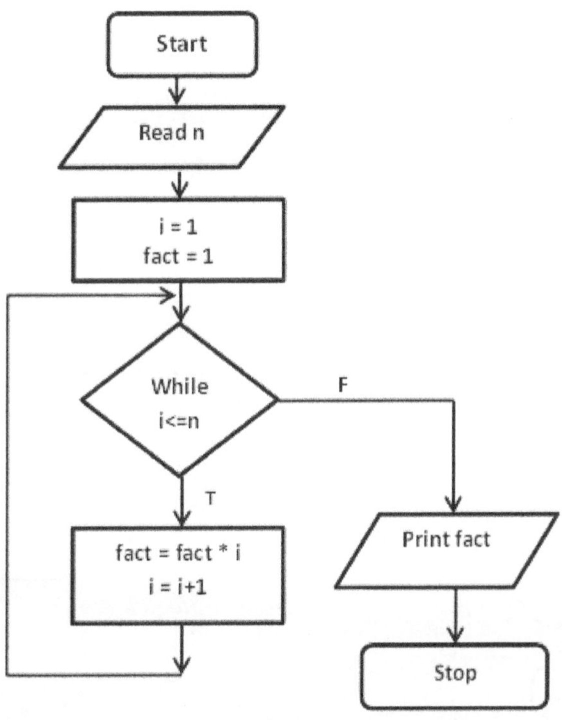

Fig. 1.19

b) Recursion:

Recursion is the process of calling a procedure from within itself, i.e., the function is called by itself again and again until some condition is satisfied. It is called as recursive function.

Example 1.12: Factorial of a number using functions

Algorithm for main program:

STEP 1: Start

STEP 2: Read the value of n

STEP 3: Call the function fact(n) and store the result in the variable 'res'

STEP 4: Print res

STEP 5: Stop

Algorithm for function fact(n)

STEP 1: Function fact (n) start

STEP 2: if n==0, then return 1, else goto step 3

STEP 3: return (n*fact (n-1))

Pseudocode:

```
Main program
    READ n
    res = CALL the function fact (n)
    PRINT res
Function fact (n)
    IF n==0 THEN
            RETURN 1
    ELSE
            RETURN n*fact (n-1)
    ENDIF
```

Flowchart

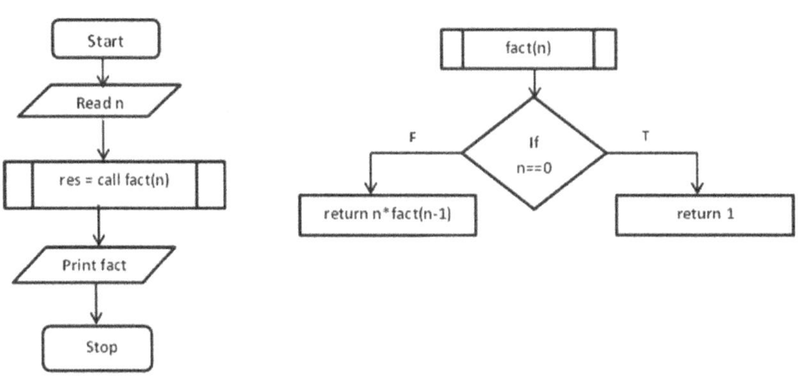

Fig. 1.20

Advantages

1. Code looks clean and elegant.
2. Complex task divided into simpler sub-problems
3. Sequence generation is easier with recursion

Disadvantages

1. Logic behind recursion is hard to follow.
2. Hard to debug
3. Recursion calls are expensive

The differences between recursion and iteration:

Table 1.8

Recursion	Iteration
1. Uses selection structure (if, if-else)	1. Uses repetition structure (while, do-while, for)
2. Recursion makes code simpler	2. Iteration makes code longer
3. Uses more memory than iteration	3. Consumes less memory compared to recursion
4. Recursion is slower than iteration due to overhead of maintaining stack	4. It does not use stack
5. Terminates when a base condition is satisfied	5. Terminates when the loop condition fails
6. Recursion function is a function that is partially defined by itself	6. Iterative instructions are loop-based repetition of a process
7. Infinite recursion occurs if the recursion step does not reduce the problem in a manner that converges on some condition	7. If the loop condition is always true then it will be an infinite loop

1.6 ILLUSTRATIVE PROBLEMS

1.6.1: Find the minimum in a list

Problem Description:

The Minimum in a list of elements can be found in two different ways:

i. Sort the list of elements in ascending order and get the first element as the minimum. (OR)

ii. Compare each element in the list and find the minimum element. This procedure will be followed in this example.

Procedure:

i) Assume the first element as the minimum element and start comparing with the next (second) element.

ii) If the next element is smaller, then assume the second element as the minimum and keep repeating the procedure till the last element.

Algorithm:

Step 1: Start the program

Step 2: Read the total number of elements 'n' in a list 'a'

Step 3: Repeat the loop for i = 0 to n-1

Step 3.1: Read the elements a[i] (*a[0] being the first element*)

Step 4: min = a[0]

Step 5: Repeat the loop for i = 1 to n-1

Step 5.1: if a[i]<min
    min = a[i]

Step 6: Print min

Step 7: Stop

Pseudocode:

```
BEGIN
    READ n
    FOR i = 0 to n-1
            READ a[i]
    ENDFOR
    SET min = a[0]
    FOR i = 1 to n-1
            IF a[i]<min THEN
                    min = a[i]
            ENDIF
    ENDFOR
    PRINT min
END
```

Procedure decoding:

n = 3

a = [3, 4, 1]

min = a[0] i.e., min = 3

for i = 1 to 2

i = 1, a[1]<min i.e., 4<3 false

i = 2, a[2]<min i.e., 1<3 true, min=1

Output: 1

1.6.2: Insert a card in a list of sorted cards

Problem Description:

Read the list of sorted cards.
Read the new card
Find the position of new card and place the new card.

Algorithm:

```
Step 1: Start
Step 2: Read 'n', the total number of cards in a list 'a'
Step 3: Read a list 'a' with n number of cards in a sorted order (ascending)
Step 4: Read newcard
Step 5: i = n-1
Step 6: Repeat Step 6.1 until i>=0
Step 6.1: if newcard < a[i]
                  a[i+1] = a[i]
                  i = i-1
          else
                  a[i+1] = newcard
Step 7: Repeat Step 7.1 for i = 0 to n
              7.1 Print a[i]
Step 8: Stop
```

Pseudocode:

```
BEGIN
READ n
FOR i = 0 to n-1
    READ a[i]
ENDFOR
READ newcard
SET i = n-1
WHILE i>=0 DO
    IF newcard<a[i] THEN
            SET a[i+1] = a[i]
            DECREMENT i
    ELSE
    SET a[i+1] = newcard
    ENDIF
ENDWHILE
FOR i = 0 to n
    PRINT a[i]
ENDFOR
END
```

Procedure decoding:

```
n = 3
a = [10, 20, 30]
newcard = 15
i = 2
2>=0 true
    15<a[2] i.e., 15<30 true
    a[3]=30   a=[10, 20, ,30]
i =1
    15<20 true
    a[2]=20   a=[10, 20, 30]
i =0
    15<10 false
    a[1]=15   a=[10, 15, 20, 30]
```

1.6.3: Guess an integer number in a range:

Problem Description:

i. Get the guess number as input.
ii. Choose a random number in a range
iii. Then compare the guessed number with the chosen random number. If they are equal, then print 'correct guess' else if the guessed number is greater than the chosen random number, then print "Your guess is too High" else print "Your guess is too low".

Algorithm:

```
Step 1: Start
Step 2: Read a number 'guess'
Step 3: hidden = choose a random number in a range
Step 4: if guess == hidden
                print "Correct Guess "
        else if guess > hidden
                print "Your guess is too High"
        else
                print "Your guess is too low"
Step 5: Stop.
```

Pseudocode:

```
READ guess
SET hidden = choose a random number in a range
```

```
IF guess == hidden THEN
        PRINT "Correct Guess"
ELSE IF guess > hidden THEN
        PRINT "Your guess is too High"
ELSE
        PRINT "Your guess is too low"
ENDIF
```

Procedure decoding:

guess = 25
hidden = 10
If 25 == 10 false
else if 25>10 true

Output: Your guess is too High

1.6.4: Towers of Hanoi

A **Towers of Hanoi** is an example illustrating the recursion technique. It consists of three towers such as source, auxiliary and destination. One or more disks (n) are stacked on towers in ascending order. Move n disks from source to destination without violating the sequence.

If it has 'n' disks then 2^n-1 movements are needed.

The movement of the disks is restricted by the following rules:

1. Only one disk can be moved from source to destination tower through auxiliary tower
2. Only the "top" disk can be removed
3. No large disk can be placed over a small disk

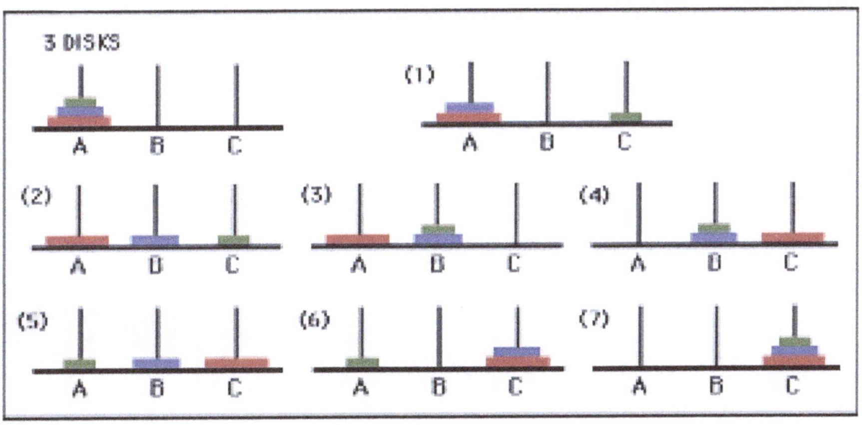

Fig. 1.21

Algorithm:

n – number of disks, A – source, C – destination, B – auxiliary

Tower of Hanoi (n,A,B,C)

Step 1: If only one disk (n==1) is there, then move disk from A to C directly.

Step 2: If more disks are there (n>1) then

Step 2.1: Recursively call the function Towerof Hanoi (n-1, A, C, B)

Step 2.2: Move nth disk from A to C

Step 2.3: Recursively call Towerof Hanoi (n-1, B, A, C)

Step 3: Stop

Pseudocode:

```
n – number of disks
A – source
B – auxiliary
C – destination
PROCEDURE TOWEROFHANOI (n, A, B, C)
    IF n==1, THEN
        Move disk from A to C
    ELSE
        CALL TOWEROFHANOI (n-1, A, C, B)
        Move nth disk from A to B
        CALL TOWEROFHANOI (n-1, B, A, C)
    ENDIF
END PROCEDURE
```

Solved Problems

Prob 1: Develop Algorithm, write Pseudocode and draw Flowchart for a procedure to add two numbers. (AU, *Jan 2018*)

Ans:

a. **Algorithm:**

Step 1: Start

Step 2: Read two values A and B

Step 3: Add A and B and store the value in C

Step 4: Print the value of C

Step 5: Stop

b. **Pseudocode:**

```
BEGIN
        READ A, B
        COMPUTE   C=A + B
        PRINT C
END
```

c. **Flowchart**

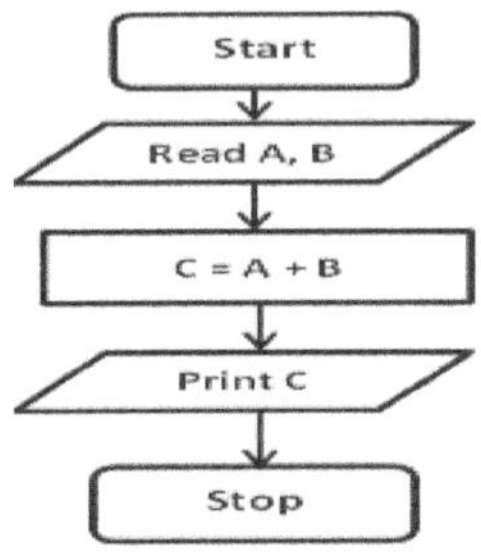

Fig. 1.22

Prob 2: Develop Algorithm, write Pseudocode and draw Flowchart for a procedure to find the area and circumference of a circle.

Ans:

a. **Algorithm:**

Step 1: Start

Step 2: Read radius of the circle r

Step 3: Compute area = 3.14 * r * r, circum = 2 * 3.14 * r

Step 4: Print area, circum

Step 5: Stop

b. **Pseudocode:**

```
BEGIN
        READ r
        COMPUTE area = 3.14 * r * r
        COMPUTE circum = 2 * 3.14 * r
        PRINT area, circum
END
```

c. **Flowchart**

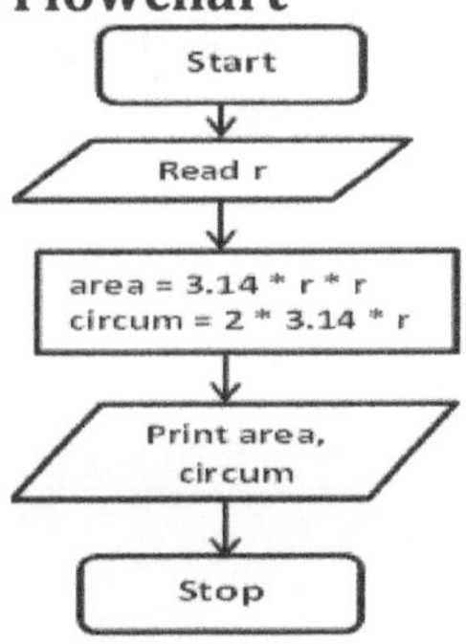

Fig. 1.23

Prob 3: Develop Algorithm, write Pseudocode and draw Flowchart for a procedure to Convert Celsius to Fahrenheit.

Ans:

a. **Algorithm:**

Step 1: Start

Step 2: Read celsius value C

Step 3: Calculate the fahrenheit value F = (9 / 5 * C) + 32

Step 4: Print the fahrenheit value F

Step 5: Stop

b. **Pseudocode:**

```
BEGIN
        READ C
        COMPUTE F = (9 / 5 * C) + 32
        PRINT F
END
```

c. Flowchart

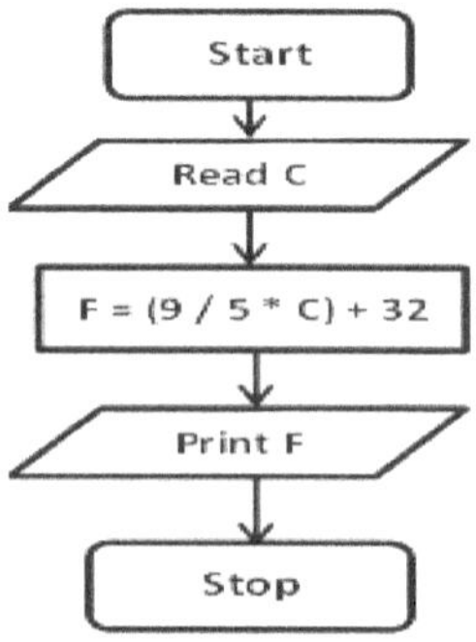

Fig. 1.24

Prob 4: Develop Algorithm, write Pseudocode and draw Flowchart for a procedure to swap two numbers.

Ans:

a. **Algorithm:**

Step 1: Start

Step 2: Read the values 'x' and 'y'

Step 3: Assign the value 'x' to the variable 'temp'

Step 4: Assign the value 'y' to the variable 'x'

Step 5: Assign the value 'temp' to the variable 'y'

Step 6: Print x and y

Step 7: Stop

b. **Pseudocode:**

```
BEGIN
        READ x, y
        SET temp = x
        SET x = y
        SET y = temp
        PRINT x and y
END
```

c. **Flowchart**

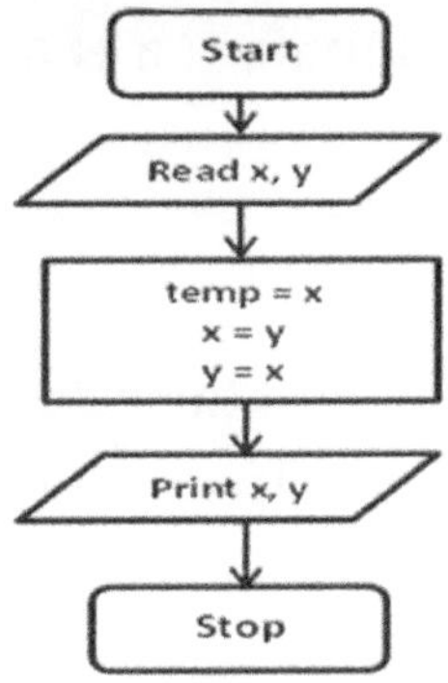

Fig. 1.25

Prob 5: Develop Algorithm, write Pseudocode and draw Flowchart for a procedure to swap two numbers without using third variable.

Ans:

a. **Algorithm:**

Step 1: Start
Step 2: Read the values 'x' and 'y'
Step 3: Add x and y then store to x
Step 4: Subtract y from x then store to y
Step 5: Subtract y from x then store to x
Step 6: Print x and y values
Step 7: Stop

b. **Pseudocode:**

```
BEGIN
        READ x, y
        COMPUTE x = x + y
        COMPUTE y = x - y
        COMPUTE x = x - y
        PRINT x, y
END
```

c. **Flowchart**

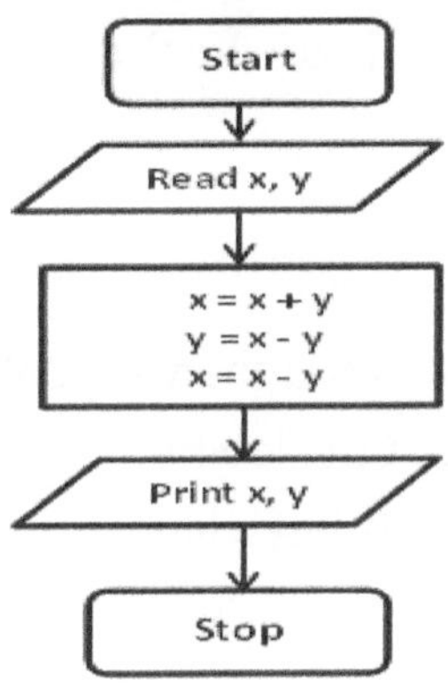

Fig. 1.26

Prob 6: Develop Algorithm, write Pseudocode and draw Flowchart for a procedure to find area of a triangle given all three sides.

Ans:

a. **Algorithm:**

Step 1: Start

Step 2: Read the values for sides of a triangle a, b, c

Step 3: Compute s = (a + b + c) / 2

Step 4: Compute d = (s * (s - a) * (s - b) * (s - c))

Step 5: Compute area = d ** 0.5

Step 6: Print area

Step 7: Stop

b. **Pseudocode:**

```
BEGIN
        READ a, b, c
        COMPUTE s = (a + b + c) / 2
        COMPUTE d = (s * (s - a) * (s - b) * (s - c))
        COMPUTE area = d ** 0.5
        PRINT area
END
```

c. **Flowchart**

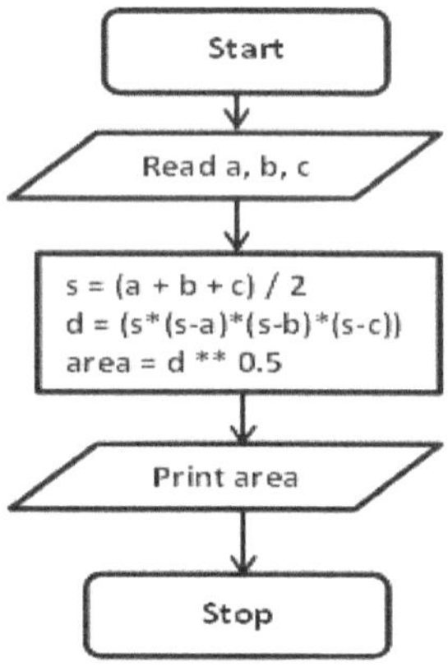

Fig. 1.27

Prob 7: Develop Algorithm, write Pseudocode and draw Flowchart for a procedure to find whether a given number is positive or not.

Ans:

a. **Algorithm:**

Step 1: Start

Step 2: Read the value of a

Step 3: Check whether 'a' is greater than or equal to zero. If yes, goto step 4 otherwise, goto step 5

Step 4: Print 'Positive' then goto step 6

Step 5: Print 'Negative'

Step 6: Stop

b. Pseudocode:

```
BEGIN
        READ a
        IF (a>=0) THEN
                PRINT "Positive"
        ELSE
                PRINT "Negative"
        ENDIF
END
```

c. Flowchart

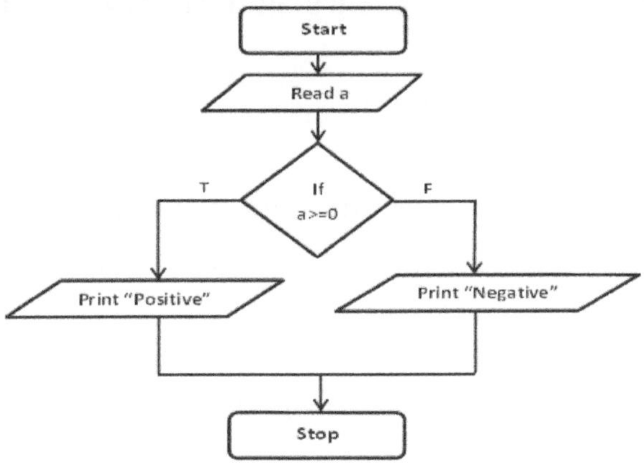

Fig. 1.28

Prob 8: Develop Algorithm, write Pseudocode and draw Flowchart for a procedure to check whether the given number is odd or even.

Ans:

a. Algorithm:

Step 1: Start

Step 2: Read the value of a

Step 3: Compute and check whether the value of a%2 is equal to zero. If yes, then goto step 4, otherwise goto step 5

Step 4: Print "Even" then goto step 6

Step 5: Print "Odd"

Step 6: Stop

b. Pseudocode:

```
BEGIN
        READ a
        IF (a % 2 == 0) THEN
                PRINT "Even"
        ELSE
                PRINT "Odd"
        ENDIF
END
```

c. Flowchart

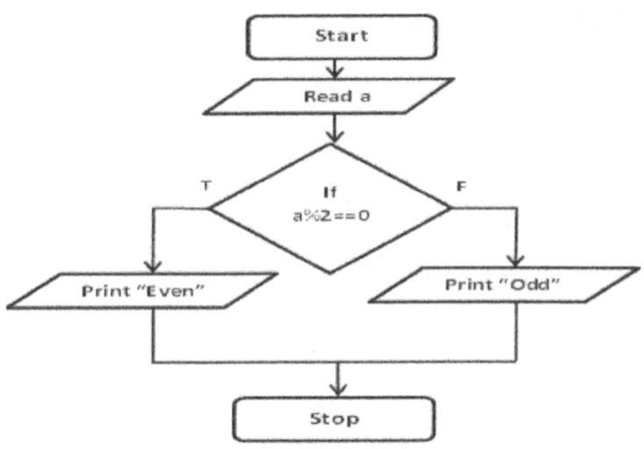

Fig. 1.29

Prob 9: Develop Algorithm, write Pseudocode and draw Flowchart for a procedure to find the greater of two numbers.

Ans:

a. **Algorithm:**

Step 1: Start

Step 2: Read the value of x and y

Step 3: Compare x and y, if x is greater than y, then goto step 4 otherwise, goto step 5

Step 4: Print "x is greater" then goto step 6

Step 5: Print "y is greater"

Step 6: Stop

b. **Pseudocode:**

```
BEGIN
        READ x, y
        IF (x>y) THEN
                PRINT "x is greater"
        ELSE
                PRINT "y is greater"
        ENDIF
END
```

c. **Flowchart**

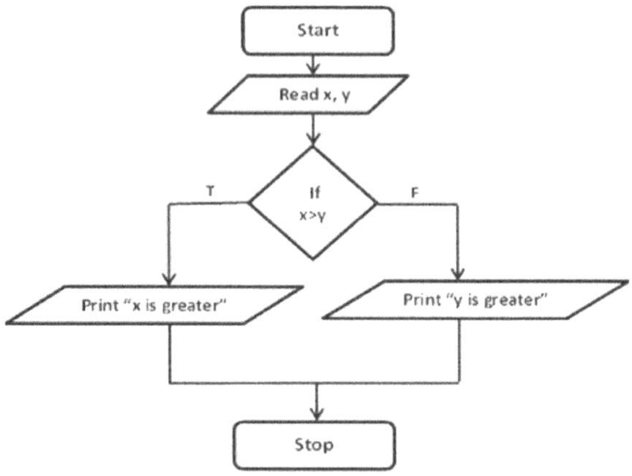

Fig. 1.30

Prob 10: Develop Algorithm, write Pseudocode and draw Flowchart for a procedure to compute the sum of first 100 natural numbers.

Ans:

a. **Algorithm:**

Step 1: Start

Step 2: Initialize sum=0, i=1

Step 3: Repeat the following steps 3.1 and 3.2 until the condition i<=100 is true

Step 3.1: sum=sum + i

Step 3.2: i = i + 1

Step 4: Print the value of sum

Step 5: Stop

b. Pseudocode:

```
BEGIN
    INITIALIZE sum=0, i=1
    WHILE (i<=100) DO
            COMPUTE sum = sum + i
            COMPUTE i = i + 1
    ENDWHILE
    PRINT sum
END
```

c. Flowchart

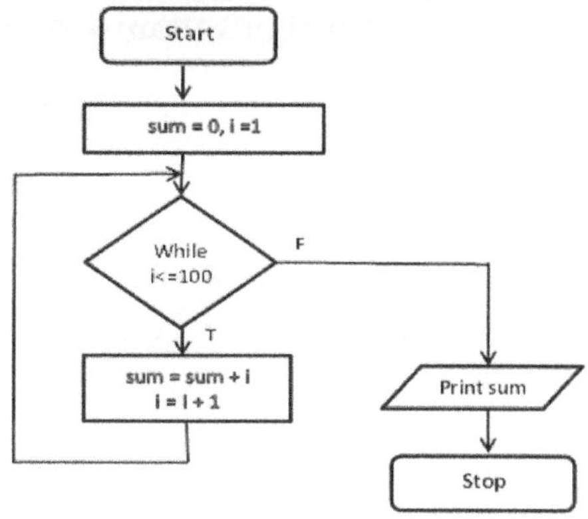

Fig. 1.31

Prob 11: Develop Algorithm, write Pseudocode and draw Flowchart for a procedure to sum the odd numbers from 1 to 100.

Ans:

a. Algorithm:

Step 1: Start

Step 2: Initialize sum=0, i=1

Step 3: Repeat the following steps 3.1 and 3.2 until the condition i<=100 is true

Step 3.1: sum=sum + i

Step 3.2: i = i + 2

Step 4: Print the value of sum

Step 5: Stop

b. Pseudocode:

```
BEGIN
    INITIALIZE sum=0, i=1
    WHILE (i<100) DO
            COMPUTE sum = sum + i
            COMPUTE i = i + 2
    ENDWHILE
    PRINT sum
END
```

c. Flowchart

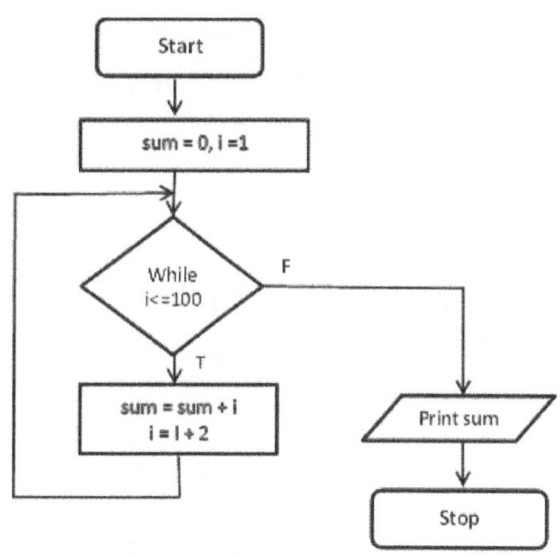

Fig. 1.32

Prob 12: Develop Algorithm, write Pseudocode and draw Flowchart for a procedure to print numbers from 1 to 10.

Ans:

a. Algorithm:

Step 1: Start

Step 2: Assign zero to count

Step 3: Calculate count = count + 1

Step 4: Print count

Step 5: Check whether count<10, If yes, goto step 3 else goto step 6

Step 6: Stop

b. Pseudocode:

```
BEGIN
    INITIALIZE count = 0
    DO
            COMPUTE count = count + 1
            PRINT count
    WHILE (count<10)
END
```

c. Flowchart

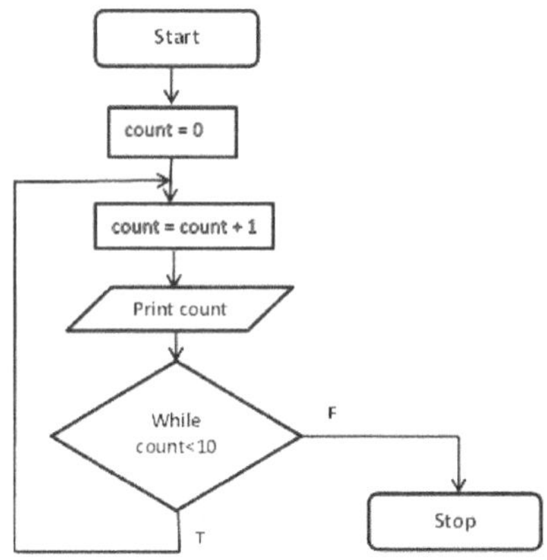

Fig. 1.33

Prob 13: Develop Algorithm, write Pseudocode and draw Flowchart for a procedure to check whether the given year is leap year or not.

Ans:

a. Algorithm:

Step 1: Start

Step 2: Read a year

Step 3: Compare and check whether the value of year%4 is equal to zero. If yes, then goto step 4 else goto step 5

Step 4: Print "Leap year"

Step 5: Print "Not a leap year"

Step 6: Stop

b. Pseudocode:

```
BEGIN
    READ year
    IF (year%4 ==0) THEN
            PRINT "Leap year"
    ELSE
            PRINT "Not a leap year"
    ENDIF
END
```

c. Flowchart

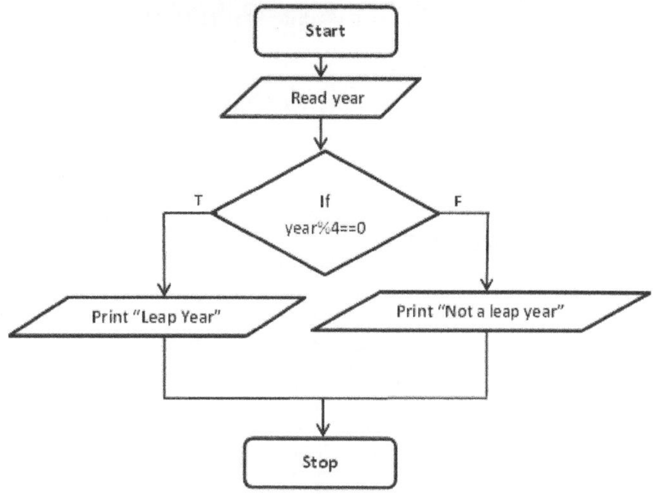

Fig. 1.34

Prob 14: Develop Algorithm, write Pseudocode and draw Flowchart for a procedure to check whether the given number is palindrome or not.

Ans:

a. **Algorithm:**

Step 1: Start

Step 2: Read the value of num integer

Step 3: Initialize rev = 0, temp = num

Step 4: Repeat the following steps until num!=0

  Step 4.1: digit = num % 10

  Step 4.2: rev = rev * 10 + digit

  Step 4.3: num = num / 10

Step 5: Compare temp and rev, if it is equal then display "Palindrome" otherwise display "Not Palindrome"

Step 6: Stop

b. **Pseudocode**

```
BEGIN
        READ num
        INITIALIZE rev = 0, temp = num
        WHILE (num!=0) DO
                COMPUTE digit = num % 10
                COMPUTE rev = rev * 10 + digit
                COMPUTE num = num / 10
        ENDWHILE
```

```
        IF (temp==rev) THEN
                PRINT "Palindrome"
        ELSE
                PRINT "Not Palindrome"
        ENDIF
    END
```

c. **Flowchart**

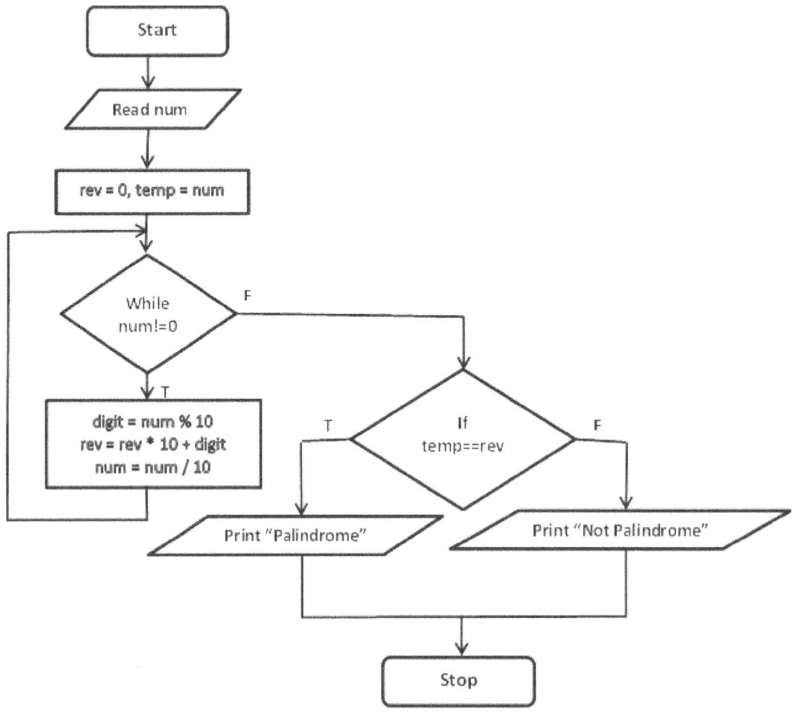

Fig. 1.35

Prob 15: Develop Algorithm, write Pseudocode and draw Flowchart for a procedure to check whether the given three digit number is Armstrong number or not. ***(An Armstrong number of three digits is an integer such that the sum of cubes of its digits is equal to the number itself. For Example $153=1^3+5^3+3^3$, $371=3^3+7^3+1^3$)***

Ans:

a. **Algorithm:**

Step 1: Start

Step 2: Read the value of num

Step 3: Initialize sum = 0, temp = num

Step 4: Repeat the following steps until num!=0

Step 4.1: digit = num % 10

Step 4.2: sum = sum + digit * digit * digit

Step 4.3: num = num / 10

Step 5: Compare temp and sum, if it is equal then display "Armstrong" otherwise display "Not Armstrong"

Step 6: Stop

b. Pseudocode

```
BEGIN
        READ num
        INITIALIZE sum = 0, temp = num
        WHILE (num!=0) DO
                COMPUTE digit = num % 10
                COMPUTE sum = sum + digit * digit * digit
                COMPUTE num = num / 10
        ENDWHILE
        IF (temp==sum) THEN
                PRINT "Armstrong"
        ELSE
                PRINT "Not Armstrong"
        ENDIF
END
```

c. Flowchart

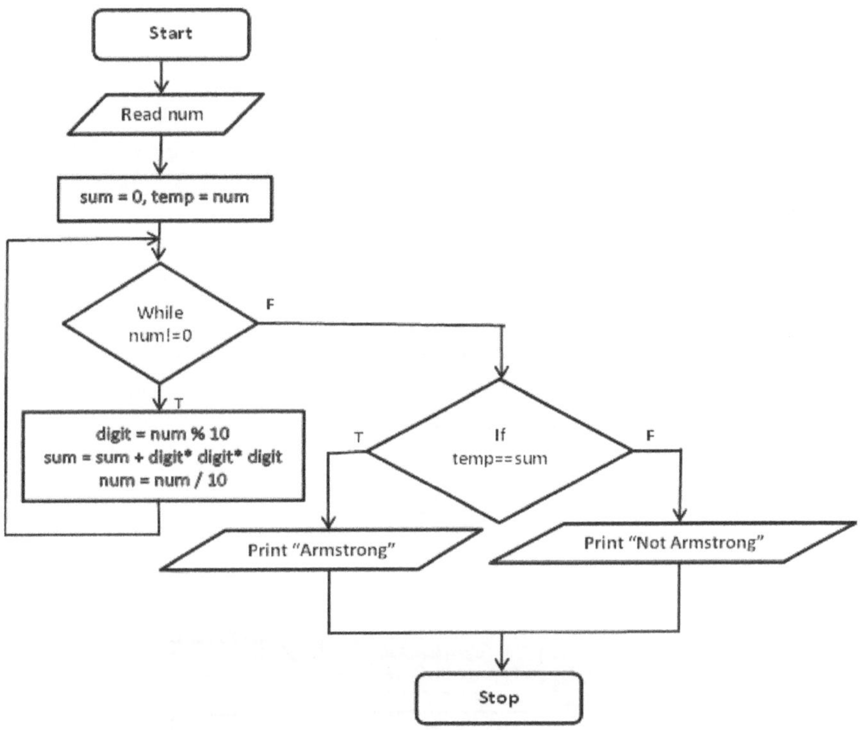

Fig. 1.36

Prob 16: Develop Algorithm, write Pseudocode and draw Flowchart for a procedure to find the sum of digits of a given number.

Ans:

a. **Algorithm:**

Step 1: Start

Step 2: Read the value of num

Step 3: Initialize sum = 0

Step 4: Repeat the following steps until num!=0

Step 4.1: digit = num % 10

Step 4.2: sum = sum + digit

Step 4.3: num = num / 10

Step 5: Print sum

Step 6: Stop

b. **Pseudocode**

```
BEGIN
        READ num
        INITIALIZE sum = 0
        WHILE (num!=0) DO
                COMPUTE digit = num % 10
                COMPUTE sum = sum + digit
                COMPUTE num = num / 10
        ENDWHILE
        PRINT sum
END
```

c. **Flowchart**

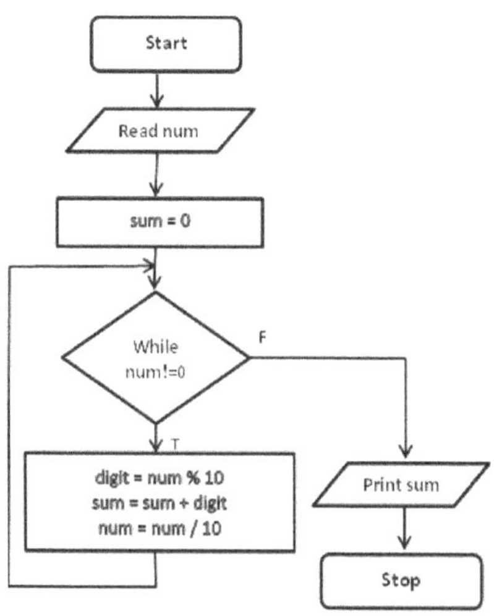

Fig. 1.37

Prob 17: Develop Algorithm, write Pseudocode and draw Flowchart for a procedure to reverse a given number.

Ans:

a. **Algorithm:**

Step 1: Start

Step 2: Read the value of num

Step 3: Initialize rev = 0

Step 4: Repeat the following steps until num!=0

  Step 4.1: digit = num % 10

  Step 4.2: rev = rev * 10 + digit

  Step 4.3: num = num / 10

Step 5: Display rev

Step 6: Stop

b. **Pseudocode**

```
BEGIN
        READ num
        INITIALIZE rev = 0
        WHILE (num!=0) DO
                COMPUTE digit = num % 10
                COMPUTE rev = rev * 10 + digit
                COMPUTE num = num / 10
        ENDWHILE
        PRINT rev
END
```

c. **Flowchart**

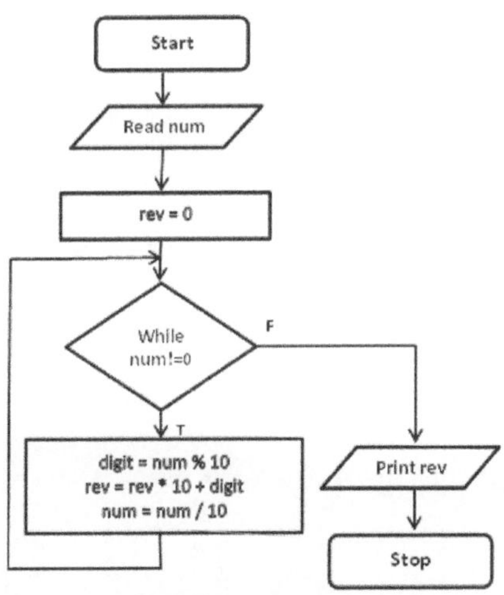

Fig. 1.38

Prob 18: Develop Algorithm, write Pseudocode and draw Flowchart for a procedure to check whether the given number is prime or not.

Ans:

a. **Algorithm:**

Step 1: Start

Step 2: Read the value of num

Step 3: Initialize i = 2, flag = 0

Step 4: Repeat the following steps until i<num

Step 4.1: check if num % i is equal to zero then set flag is 1, break; else i = i+1

Step 5: If flag is zero then display "Prime" otherwise display "Not Prime"

Step 6: Stop

b. **Pseudocode**

```
BEGIN
        READ num
        INITIALIZE i = 2, flag = 0
        WHILE (i<num) DO
                IF (num % i == 0) THEN
                        SET flag = 1
                        BREAK
                ELSE
                        i = i +1
                ENDIF
        ENDWHILE
        IF (flag==0) THEN
                PRINT "Prime"
        ELSE
        PRINT "Not Prime"
        ENDIF
END
```

c. **Flowchart**

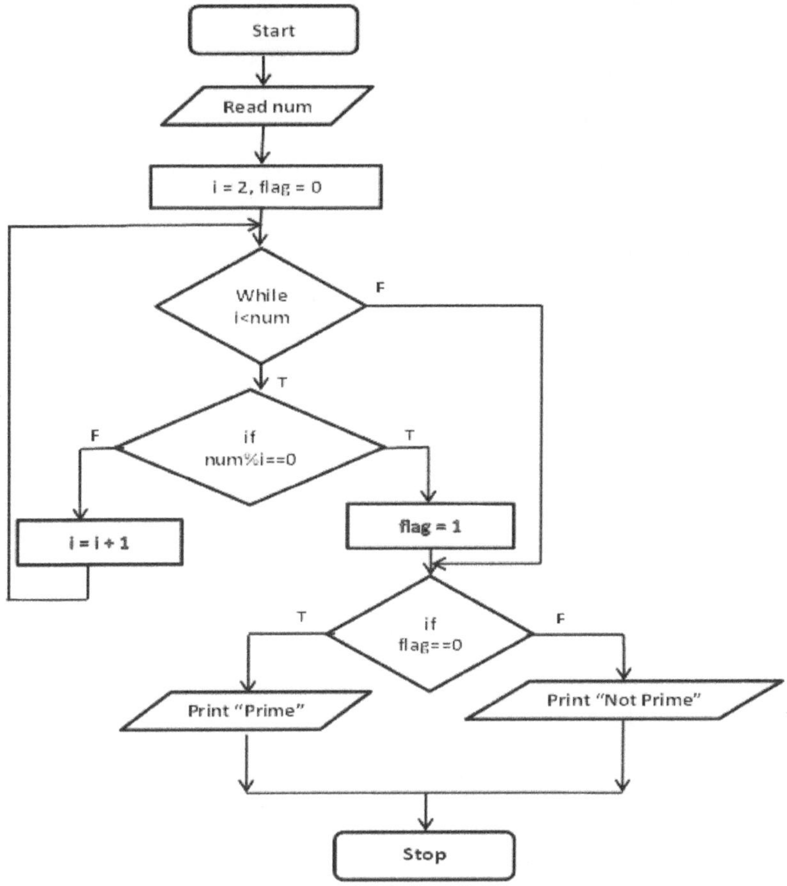

Fig. 1.39

Prob 19: Develop Algorithm, write Pseudocode and draw Flowchart for a procedure to generate the Fibonacci series. ***(The Fibonacci Series is 0, 1, 1, 2, 3, 5, 8, 13, 21, ...)***

Ans:

a. **Algorithm:**

Step 1: Start

Step 2: Read the value of 'n'

Step 3: Initialize count = 1, f1 = -1, f2 = 1

Step 4: Repeat the following steps until count<=n

  Step 4.1: calculate f3 = f1 + f2

  Step 4.2: Display f3

  Step 4.3: Assign f1 =f2, f2 =f3

  Step 4.4: count = count + 1

Step 5: Stop

b. Pseudocode

```
BEGIN
        READ n
        INITIALIZE count = 1, f1 = -1, f2 = 1
        WHILE (count<=n) DO
                COMPUTE f3 =f1 + f2
                PRINT f3
                SET f1 = f2, f2 = f3
                INCREMENT count = count +1
        ENDWHILE
END
```

c. Flowchart

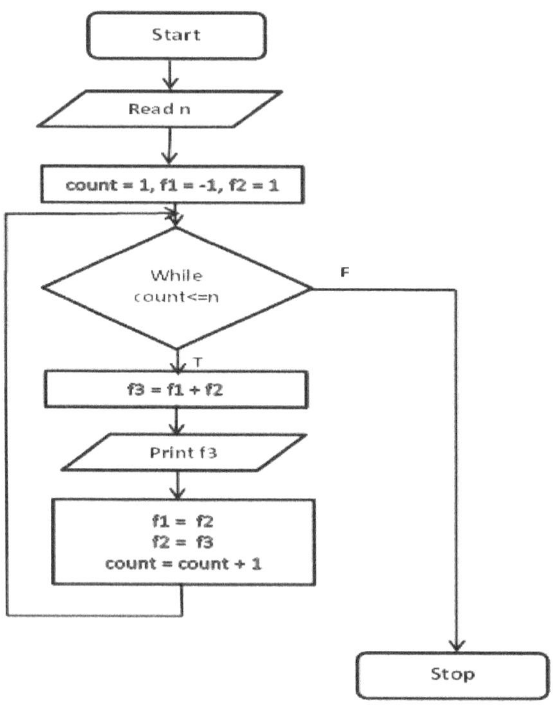

Fig. 1.40

Short Questions

1. What is an algorithm? (AU, *Jan 2018*)

Algorithm is an ordered sequence of finite, well-defined, and unambiguous instructions to solve a given problem and produce a desired result for given input in a finite amount of time. It is a step-by-step procedure for solving a problem.

2. Write an algorithm to find the minimum of 3 given numbers.

Algorithm: Find the Minimum of 3 given numbers

Step 1: Start

Step 2: Read the three numbers A, B, C

Step 3: Compare A and B.
If A is less then go to step 4 else go to step 5.

Step 4: Compare A and C. If A is less then print "A is minimum" else print "C is minimum". Go to step 6.

Step 5: Compare B and C. If B is less then print "B is minimum" else print "C is minimum".

Step 6: Stop

3. List the building blocks of an algorithm.

The building blocks of an algorithm are

a. Statements
b. Sequence
c. Selection or Conditional
d. Repetition or Control flow
e. Functions

4. Define statement. List its types.

A **statement** is a command given to the computer to take a specific action such as: collect the input, process the input and display the output to the screen. A computer program is a series of statements.

5. Write the pseudocode to calculate the sum and product of two numbers and display them.

```
BEGIN
    INITIALIZE variables sum, product, number1, number2
    PRINT "Input two numbers"
    READ number1, number2
    COMPUTE sum = number1 + number2
    PRINT "The sum is ", sum
    COMPUTE product = number1 * number2
    PRINT "The Product is ", product
END
```

6. How does flow of control work?

Control flow (or flow of control) is the order in which individual statements, instructions or function calls of a program are executed or evaluated. A control flow statement is a statement in which the execution results in a choice being made as to which of two or more paths to follow.

7. What is a function?

Function is defined as a subprogram which contains a set of instructions to perform some specific task. Functions provide better modularity for an application and a high degree of code reusing. It is also called as methods, sub-routines and procedure.

A function is often executed several times, from several different places during a single execution of the program. After finishing a subroutine the program will return to the point from where the function is called.

8. Give the rules for writing Pseudocodes.

1 Use words that are easily translated into computer instructions.
2 Use indentation within a loop or a conditional clause.
3 Do not include data declarations in pseudo code.
4 Write one statement per line.

9. Give the difference between flowchart and pseudocode.

Flowchart and Pseudocode are used to document and represent an algorithm. In other words, an algorithm can be represented using a flowchart or a pseudocode. Flowchart is a graphical representation of the algorithm. Pseudo code is a readable, formally an English language representation of the algorithm.

10. Define a flowchart.

A flowchart is a diagrammatic representation of the logic for solving a task. A flowchart is drawn using boxes of different shapes with lines connecting them to show the flow of control. The purpose of drawing a flowchart is to make the logic of the program clearer in a visual form.

11. Give an example of iteration.

```
a = 0
for i = 1 to 3          // loop three times
{
  a = a + i            // add the current value of i to a
}
print a                // the number 6 is printed (0 + 1; 1 + 2; 3 + 3)
```

12. Write down the rules for preparing a flowchart.

While drawing a flowchart, some rules need to be followed:

- Standard symbols should only be used.
- The arrowheads in the flowchart represent the direction of flow of control.
- Flow direction is from top to bottom or left to right.
- Flow lines should not cross each other.
- Be consistent in using names and variables in the flowchart.
- Keep the flowchart as simple as possible.

- Words in the flowchart symbols should be common statements and easy to understand.
- Plan and incorporate all the details of logic related to the problem.
- If new page is needed, then use connectors.

13. List the categories of Programming languages.

Programming languages are divided into the following categories:

1. Low Level Programming Language
2. Assembly Level Programming Language
3. High Level Programming Language

14. Mention the characteristics of an algorithm.

a. Algorithm should be precise and unambiguous.
b. Instruction in an algorithm should not be repeated infinitely.
c. Algorithm should ultimately terminate.
d. Algorithm should be written in sequence.
e. Algorithm should be written in normal English.
f. Desired result should be obtained only after the algorithm terminates.

15. Compare machine language, assembly language and high-level language.

Machine language is a collection of binary digits or bits that the computer reads and interprets. This language is not easily understandable by the human.

An assembly language directly controls the physical hardware. A program written in assembly language consists of a series of instruction mnemonics that correspond to a stream of executable instructions which when translated by an assembler can be loaded into memory and executed. The programs written in this language are not portable and the debugging process is also not very easy.

A high level language is much more abstract, that must be translated or compiled into machine language. It is easily understandable. Debugging the code is easy and the program written is not machine dependent.

16. What is the difference between algorithm and pseudo code?

An algorithm is a systematic logical approach used to solve problems in a computer while pseudocode is the statement in plain English that may be translated later to a programming language. Pseudocode is the intermediary between algorithm and program.

17. List the simple steps to develop an algorithm.

Algorithm development process consists of five major steps.

Step 1: Obtain a description of the problem.

Step 2: Analyze the problem.

Step 3: Develop a high-level algorithm.

Step 4: Refine the algorithm by adding more detail.

Step 5: Review the algorithm.

18. Give the differences between recursion and iteration.

Recursion	Iteration
1. Uses selection structure (if, if-else)	1. Uses repetition structure (while, do-while, for)
2. Recursion makes code simpler. Uses more memory than iteration	2. Iteration makes code longer. Consumes less memory compared to recursion
3. Recursion is slower than iteration due to overhead of maintaining stack	3. It does not use stack
4. Terminates when a base condition is satisfied	4. Terminates when the loop condition fails
5. Recursion function is a function that is partially defined by itself	5. Iterative instructions are loop-based repetition of a process
6. Infinite recursion occurs if the recursion step does not reduce the problem in a manner that converges on some condition	6. If the loop condition is always true then it will be an infinite loop

19. What are advantages and disadvantages of recursion?

Advantages	Disadvantages
Recursive functions make the code look clean and elegant.	Sometimes the logic behind recursion is hard to follow through.
A complex task can be broken down into simpler sub-problems using recursion.	Recursive calls are expensive (inefficient) as they take up a lot of memory and time.
Sequence generation is easier with recursion than using some nested iteration.	Recursive functions are hard to debug.

20. Distinguish between algorithm and program. (AU, *Jan 2019)*

Algorithm	Program
Algorithm is an ordered sequence of finite, well-defined, and unambiguous instructions to solve a given problem and produce a desired result for given input in a finite amount of time. It is a step-by-step procedure for solving a problem.	**Program** is a sequence of instructions that tells a computer how to do a task.

Unsolved Exercises

Develop an Algorithm, write Pseudocode and draw Flowchart for the following problems:

1. To find the product of two numbers.
2. To find the average of two numbers.
3. To generate multiplication table for a given number.
4. To find the quotient and remainder of m/n, where m and n are integers.
5. To find the roots of a Quadratic equation.
6. To find the value of nPr for given value of n & r.
7. To find the value of nCr for given value of n & r.
8. To find GCD of two numbers.
9. To find LCM of two numbers.
10. To count the number of digits in an integer.
11. To calculate the area of equilateral triangle.
12. To find prime numbers in a given range.

UNIT II
DATA, EXPRESSIONS, STATEMENTS IN PYTHON

Contents

Python interpreter and interactive mode; values and types: int, float, Booleans, strings, and lists; variables, expressions, statements, tuple assignment, precedence of operators, comments; modules and functions, function definition and use, flow of execution, parameters and arguments; Illustrative programs: exchange the values of two variables, circulate the values of n variables, distance between two points.

2.1 INTRODUCTION TO PYTHON PROGRAMMING

Python programming language was created by Guido van Rossum and it was released in the early 1990s. Python name comes from a 1970s British comedy sketch television show called 'Monty Python's Flying Circus'. When van Rossum was reading about this show he thought the name Python was short, unique and a bit mysterious and would be suitable for his new language.

2.1.1 Python Language

Python is a general-purpose language. Python is a powerful high-level, object-oriented programming language which has simple easy-to-use syntax, making it the perfect language for novice user.

Python has wide range of applications from Web development (like, Django and Bottle), scientific and mathematical computing (like, Orange, SymPy, NumPy) to desktop graphical user Interfaces (like, Pygame, Panda3D).

Python has a simple syntax. The syntax of the language is clean and length of the code is relatively short. Python programs are clear and easy to read, and have less number of lines compared to other language programs. At the same time, Python provides powerful programming features and is widely used. The companies and organizations that use Python are: YouTube, Google, Yahoo and NASA.

2.1.2 Features of Python

1. A simple language which is easier to learn

Python is syntactically very simple and elegant. Programmers can focus on the solution rather than on the syntax in Python programming.

2. Free and open-source

Programmers can freely use and distribute Python, even for commercial use. It is even possible to make changes to the Python's source code on iterative basis. In each iteration, Python provides the possibility of improving successively.

3. Portability

Python programs can move from one platform to another and run without any changes. It runs on the following platforms: Windows, Mac OS X and Linux.

4. A high-level, interpreter language

In Python programming, there is no need to worry about tasks like memory management, garbage collection and so on, as in C/C++ programming. When the Python code is running, the interpreter automatically converts Python code to the machine language that the computer understands.

5. Large standard libraries to solve common tasks

Python has a number of standard libraries. It helps the programmer to reuse the code. For example: to connect MySQL database on a Web server, use MySQLdb library using *import* MySQLdb.

6. Object-oriented

Python is an Object oriented programming (OOP) language. It helps to solve a complex problem easily. With OOP, it is possible to divide complex problems into smaller sets by creating objects.

2.1.3 Applications of Python

1. Web Applications

Web Apps using frameworks and CMS (Content Management System) are created by Python. Some of the popular platforms for creating Web Apps are: Django, Flask, Pyramid. Some of the CMS sites like Reddit, Instagram, Plone and PBS are written in Python.

2. Scientific and Numeric Computing

Large number of libraries is available in Python for scientific and numeric computing. For example, SciPy and NumPy are used in general purpose computing. And, there are some specific libraries like: EarthPy for earth science, AstroPy for Astronomy and so on. Also, the language is heavily used in machine learning, data mining and deep learning.

3. Creating software Prototypes

Python is slow compared to compiled languages like C++ and Java. This is not a correct choice for limited resources and where efficiency is a must. However, Python is a good language for creating prototypes. For example: A Game's prototype can be created by using Pygame library. Then the actual game can be created by using the language like C++.

4. Good Language to Teach Programming

Python is used to teach programming to kids and novice users. It has a lot of features and capabilities. It is one of the easiest languages to learn because of its simple easy-to-use syntax.

2.1.4 Reasons to Choose Python as First Language

1. Simple and Elegant Syntax

Python Programming is a fun language. It is easier to understand and write Python code. The syntax is natural. For example:

```
a = 2
b = 3
sum = a + b
print(sum)
```

Even if the user does not have any programming experience before, the user can easily guess that this program adds two numbers and prints it.

2. Not overly strict

There is no need to define the type of a variable and also not necessary to add delimiters like semicolon at the end of a statement in Python. In Python, the programmer must follow the proper indentation. So it is easy for the beginner to understand and learn Python statements.

3. Expressiveness of the language

In Python, it is possible to write programs with greater functionality and fewer lines of code.

4. Great Community Support

Python has a large supporting community. There are numerous active forums online which can be handy if you are stuck. Some of them are:

a. Learn Python subreddit

b. Google Forum for Python

c. Python Questions - Stack Overflow

2.1.5 Run Python on Your Operating System

How to Install and Run Python in Windows

1. Go to 'Download Python' page on the official site and click **Download Python 3.6.0.**
2. After the download is completed, double-click the file and follow the instructions to install it. If Python is installed then a program called IDLE is also installed along with it. It provides graphical user interface to work with Python.
3. Without creating file a program can be run in IDLE itself like: open IDLE, copy the following code below and press enter.
   Print ("Hello, World!")
4. To create a file in IDLE, go to **File > New Window** (Shortcut: **Ctrl+N**).
5. Write Python code (For example, copy the code below) and save (Shortcut: **Ctrl+S**) with **.py** file extension like: hello.py
   Print ("Hello, World!")
6. Go to **Run > Run module** (Shortcut: **F5**) and see the output.

2.1.6 The Python Interpreter and Interactive Mode

Statements written in a high-level language are called source code or code. Source code is translated into machine language using compiler or an interpreter.

- Python is an interpreted language
- The interpreter provides an interactive environment with the language
- There are two ways to use the interpreter:

1. Interactive mode

In **interactive mode**, the program statements can be typed in the prompt so that the interpreter displays the result as:

```
>>>1+1
```

Output:

```
2
```

The prompt >>> (chevron) indicates that the interpreter is ready. This interactive mode execution is convenient for smaller programs.

2. Script mode

In **script mode**, the program can be stored in a file (eg: Notepad) and the interpreter can be used to execute the file. The python script's filename ends with **.py** extension. For larger programs, the program code can be stored as a script and executed in the future. Command to execute the script:

in UNIX - python filename.py

in Windows - filename.py

For example the following script may be stored as add.py and run as shown above

```
# Add two numbers
    a=2
    b=3
    c=a+b
    print(c)
```

Output: 5

Explanation:

Line 1: # Add two numbers

Any line starting with # in Python programming is a comment.

Line 2: a=2

Here, 'a' is a variable. You can store a value in a variable. Here, 2 is stored in this variable.

Line 3: b=3

Similarly, 3 is stored in 'b' variable.

Line 4: c=a+b

The variables a and b are added using **+** operator and the result is stored in another variable c.

Line 5: print(c)

The print() function prints the output to the screen. In this case, it prints 5 on the screen.

2.1.7 Debugging:

It is the process of rectifying the errors in the program. There are three kinds of errors.

(i) **Syntax error:** Syntax refers to the structure of the program and the rules about the structure. **Ex**: *print ("Hello, World!"* - syntax error: There is no closing parenthesis.

(ii) **Runtime error:** This error appears during runtime. **Ex**.: Divide by zero error

(iii) **Semantic error:** If this error occurs, the interpreter runs the program successfully without generating error message. But it will not produce the right output.

2.2 VALUES AND TYPES

Value is one of the basic things with which a program works: like a letter or a number.

Example:

- 1, 2 (integer)
- 'Hello! World' (String)

Function named *type* tells us what type a value is, if we are not sure of it.

We can use the *type()* function to know which class a variable or a value belongs to and the *isinstance()* function to check if an object belongs to a particular class.

```
>>> type('Hi')
<type 'str'>
>>> type(12)
<type 'int'>
>>> type(5.4)
<type 'float'>
>>>a = 2
>>>print(a, "is of type", type(a))
2 is of type <class 'int'>
>>>a = 2.0
>>>print(a, "is of type", type(a))
2.0 is of type <class 'float'>
>>>a = 1+2j
>>>print(a, "is complex number?", isinstance(1+2j,complex))
(1+2j) is complex number? True
```

2.2.1 Python identifier

Python identifier is a name used to identify a variable, function, class or other object.

Rules for identifier:

1. Identifiers can be a combination of lower-case letters(a-z) or upper-case letters(A-Z) or digits(0-9) or underscore(_).
2. Identifier should start with an alphabet or an underscore but not with digits.
3. Keywords cannot be used as an identifier.
4. Special characters are not allowed except underscore.

   Valid Identifiers: ***num, total, _b_, add1***

   Invalid Identifiers: 1x, char, x+y

Python is a case sensitive language i.e., sum and Sum are not same. (Note: Identifiers are shown in bold italic letters in the text of this book.)

2.2.2 Data Types:

Every value in Python has a data type.

In Python everything is an object. Data types are actually classes and variables are instance of these classes.

There are various data types in Python. Some of the important types are listed below.

1. Numbers (Numerical literal)
    a. Integers
    b. Floats
    c. Complex numbers
    d. Booleans
2. Lists
3. String
4. Tuple
5. Dictionaries

1. Numbers

Python's four number types are integers, floats, complex numbers, and Booleans:

- Integers: 1, –3, 42, 355, 888888888888888, –7777777777
- Floats: 3.0, 31e12, –6e-4
- Complex numbers: 3 + 2j, –4- 2j, 4.2 + 6.3j
- Booleans: True, False

We can manipulate them using the arithmetic operators: + (addition), – (subtraction), * (multiplication), / (division), ** (exponentiation), and % (modulus).

Example 2.1: (Integers)

```
>>> x = 5 + 2 - 3 * 2
>>> x
1
>>> 5 / 2
2.5
>>> 5 // 2
2
>>> 5 % 2
1
>>> 2 ** 8
256
```

Division of integers with '/' results in a float, and division of integers with '//' results in truncation. Note that integers are of unlimited size. (Note: Outputs are shown in Arial font in this book.)

Example 2.2: (float)

```
>>> x = 4.3 ** 2.4
>>> x
33.137847377716483
>>> 3.5e30 * 2.77e45
9.6950000000000002e+75
```

Example 2.3:(Complex numbers)

```
>>> (3+2j) ** (2+3j)
(0.68176651908903363-2.1207457766159625j)
>>> x = (3+2j) * (4+9j)
>>> x
(-6+35j)
>>> x.real
-6.0
>>> x.imag
35.0
```

Complex numbers consist of both a real element and an imaginary element, suffixed with *j*. In the preceding code, variable *x* is assigned to a complex number.

Its "real" part is obtained using the attribute notation ***x.real*** and the complex part by using ***x.imag***.

Example 2.4: (Booleans)

```
>>> x = False
>>> x
False
>>> not x
True
>>> y = True * 2
>>> y
2
```

Other than their representation as True and False, Booleans behave like the numbers 1 (*True*) and 0 (*False*).

2. Lists

A list can contain a mixture of other types as its elements, including strings, tuples, lists, dictionaries, functions, file objects, and any type of number. A list can be indexed from its front (0, 1, 2, ...) or back(-1, -2, -3, ...). Lists are mutable. (Note: In forward indexing the index of the first element is zero, '0').

Sub segment or *slice* of a list is referred by using slice notation ':'. It displays the values from starting index to previous of end index.

Example 2.5:

```
>>> x = ["one", "two", "three", "four"]
>>> x[0]
'one'
>>> x[2]
'three'
>>> x[-1]
'four'
>>> x[-2]
'three'
>>> x[1:-1]
['two', 'three']
>>> x[0:3]
['one', 'two', 'three']
>>> x[-2:-1]
['three']
>>> x[:3]
['one', 'two', 'three']
```

3. String

String processing is one of Python's strengths.

Strings can be delimited by single (' '), double (" "), triple single (''' '''), or triple double (""" """) quotations and can contain tab (\t) and newline (\n) characters.

Example:

```
>>> s="hello"
>>>s
'hello'
```

4. Tuple

A tuple is a sequence of values. The values can be any type, and they are indexed by integers like lists. The important difference is that tuples are immutable.

It is a comma-separated list of values enclosed within parentheses.

```
>>> t=('a','b','c','d','e')
```

5. Dictionary

Dictionary is one of the compound data types like string, list and tuple. Every element in a dictionary is a 'key-value' pair.

Example 2.6:

```
>>> empty={} #An empty dictionary can also be created
>>> a={1: 'apple',2: 'ball'}
```

2.3 VARIABLES

- A variable is a name that refers to a value.
- A variable is a location in memory used to store some data (value).
- They are given unique names to differentiate between different memory locations. The rules for writing a variable name are same as the rules for writing identifiers in Python.
- In Python, there is no provision to declare a variable before using it. A variable is automatically declared when assigning a value to it. Also there is no need to declare the type of the variable. This is handled internally according to the type of value assigned to the variable.
- An **assignment statement** creates new variables and gives them values:

Example 2.7:

```
>>> msg = 'Welcome'
>>> m = 17
>>> pi = 3.141
```

The first statement assigns a string to a new variable named ***msg***; second gives the integer 17 to ***m***; third assigns the (approximate) value of π to ***pi***.

Rules for Variable names

1. Variable name should start with a letter (a-z or A-Z) or underscore but not with digits.
2. Variable names can be arbitrarily long.
3. It is legal to use uppercase letters, but normally variable name begins with a lowercase letter.

2.3.1 Python Keywords

- Keywords are the reserved words in Python.
- Keywords cannot be used as variable name, function name or any other identifier. They are used to define the syntax and structure of the Python language.
- In Python, keywords are case sensitive.
- All the keywords except *True, False* and *None* are in lowercase and they must be written as it is. (Note: Keywords and built-in functions are shown in italics in the text of this book.)

A list of keywords is given below:

Table 2.1

None	*continue*	*for*	*lambda*	*try*
True	*def*	*from*	*nonlocal*	*while*
and	*del*	*global*	*not*	*with*
as	*elif*	*if*	*or*	*yield*
assert	*else*	*import*	*pass*	
break	*except*	*in*	*raise*	

2.3.2 Python Identifiers

Python identifier is a name used to identify a variable, function, class or other object. It helps us to differentiate one entity from another.

Rules for identifier:

1. Identifiers can be a combination of lower-case letters(a-z) or upper-case letters(A-Z) or digits(0-9) or underscore(_).
2. Identifier should start with an alphabet or an underscore but not with digits.
3. Keywords cannot be used as an identifier.

   Example 2.8:

   ```
   >>> global = 1
   File "<interactive input>", line 1
   global = 1
   ^
   SyntaxError: invalid syntax
   ```

4. Special symbols are not allowed except underscore.

   Example 2.9:

   ```
   >>> a@ = 0
   File "<interactive input>", line 1
   ```

```
a@ = 0
 ^
SyntaxError: invalid syntax
```

5. Identifier can be of any length.
   Valid Identifiers: num, total, _b_, add1
   Invalid Identifiers: 1x, char, x+y
   Python is a case sensitive language i.e., sum and Sum are not same.

2.3.3 Variable assignment

Assignment operator (=) is used to assign values to a variable. Any type of value can be assigned to any valid variable.

```
a = 15
b = 5.2
c = "Hello"
```

Here, there are three assignment statements. 15 is an integer assigned to the variable ***a***. Similarly, 5.2 is a floating point number and "Hello" is a string (sequence of characters) assigned to the variables ***b*** and ***c*** respectively.

Multiple assignments

In Python, multiple assignments can be made in a single statement as follows:

```
a, b, c = 15, 5.2, "Hello"
```

This statement assigns 15 to ***a***, 5.2 to ***b***, and "Hello" to ***c***.

If the programmer wants to assign the same value to multiple variables at once, then they can do this as:

```
x = y = z = "same"
```

This assigns the "same" string to all the three variables.

2.4 EXPRESSIONS

An **expression** is a combination of operands and operators.

A value all by itself is considered an expression.

```
>>>1+2
  3
>>>x=10
>>>x++
```

A literal evaluates to itself, whereas a variable reference evaluates to the variable's current value.

Expressions provide a way to perform operations on data values to produce other data values. When entered at the Python shell prompt, an expression's operands are evaluated, and the operator is then applied to these values to compute the value of the expression.

2.4.1 Arithmetic Expressions

An **arithmetic expression** consists of operands and arithmetic operators such as addition, subtraction, multiplication, division, remainder or modulus, exponentiation, and quotient.

The following table shows several arithmetic operators used in Python code.

Table 2.2

Operator	Meaning	Python Code
+	Addition	a+b
-	Subtraction	a-b
*	Multiplication	a*b
/	Division	a/b
//	Quotient or Floor Division	a//b
%	Remainder or Modulus	a%b
**	Exponentiation	a**b
-	Negation	-a

If the expression contains more than one operator then the following **precedence rules** are applied during the evaluation of arithmetic expressions in Python:

1. Exponentiation has the highest precedence and is evaluated first.
2. Unary negation is evaluated next, before multiplication, division, and remainder.
3. Multiplication, both types of division, and remainder are evaluated before addition and subtraction.
4. Addition and subtraction are evaluated before assignment.
5. With two exceptions, operators of equal precedence are **left associative**, so they are evaluated from left to right. Exponentiation and assignment operations are **right associative**, so consecutive instances of these are evaluated from right to left.
6. Parentheses are used to change the order of evaluation.

Examples:

Table 2.3

Expression	Evaluation	Value
8+3*4	8+12	20
(8+3)*4	11*4	44
13%4	1	1
3*2**3	3*8	24
-3**2	-(3**2)	-9
3**2**3	3**8	6561
(3**2)**3	9**3	729
12/0	ZeroDivisionError: division by zero	
12%0	ZeroDivisionError: integer division or modulo by zero	

2.4.2 Mixed-Mode Arithmetic and Type Conversions

Performing calculations with both integers and floating-point numbers is called **mixed-mode arithmetic**.

For instance, if a circle has radius 3, the area may be computed as follows:

```
>>>3.14*3**2
28.26
```

Python has different operators for quotient division and exact division.

For instance,

3 // 2 * 5.0 yields **1 * 5.0**, which yields **5.0**

Whereas

3 / 2 * 5 yields **1.5 * 5**, which yields **7.5**

A **type conversion** function is a function with the same name as the data type to which it converts. Because the input function returns a string as its value, then the function *int* or *float* is used to convert the string to a number before performing arithmetic, as in the following example:

```
>>>int('10')+20
30
```

Table 2.4

Conversion Function	Example	Value returned
int(<a number or a string)	int(2.55) int("10")	2 10
float(<a number or a string)	float(12)	12.0
str(<any value>	str(9)	'9'

- The *int* function converts a *float* to an *int* by truncation, not by rounding to the nearest whole number.
- Truncation simply chops the number's fractional part.
- The *round* function rounds a *float* to the nearest *int* as in the next example:

```
>>>int(3.75)
3
>>>round(3.75)
4
```

- Another use of type conversion occurs in the construction of strings from numbers and other strings. For instance, assume that the variable ***profit*** refers to a floating-point number that represents an amount of money in dollars.
- Suppose that, it is needed to build a string that represents this value for output, and to concatenate the **$** symbol to the value of ***profit***.
- Python does not allow the use of the **+** operator with a string and a number:

```
>>> profit=1000
>>> print('$'+profit)
Traceback (most recent call last):
File "<pyshell#31>", line 1, in <module>
print('$'+profit)
TypeError: can only concatenate str (not "int") to str
```

- To solve this problem, the str function is used to convert the value of ***profit*** to a string and then concatenate this string to the $ symbol, as follows:

```
>>> print('$'+str(profit))
$1000
```

- Python is a strongly typed programming language. The interpreter checks the data types of all the operands before operators are applied to those operands. If the type of the operand is not appropriate, the interpreter halts execution with an error message.

2.5 STATEMENTS

Instructions that a Python interpreter can execute are called **statements**. For example, a = 1 is an assignment statement. A statement is a unit of code that the interpreter executes.

For Example:

```
x=2 # assignment statement
print x #print statement
```

Output:

```
2
```

The important difference between an expression and a statement is that an expression has a value; a statement does not.

2.5.1 Multi-line statement

In Python, end of a statement is marked by a newline character. But a statement can extend over multiple lines with the line continuation character (\).

For example:

```
a = 1 + 2 + 3 + \
4 + 5 + 6 + \
7 + 8 + 9
```

This is an explicit line continuation. In Python, line continuation is implied inside parentheses ( ), brackets [ ] and braces { }. For instance, the above multi-line statement can be implemented as:

```
a = (1 + 2 + 3 +
4 + 5 + 6 +
7 + 8 + 9)
```

Here, the line continuation can be implicitly done by parentheses ( ). Same in the case of [] and { }. For example:

```
colors = ['red',
'blue',
'green']
```

Multiple statements can be put in a single line using semicolons, as follows:

```
a = 1; b = 2; c = 3
```

2.5.2 Tuple Assignment

Tuple is a set of comma-separated values. Python allows a tuple of variables on the left of an assignment operator and values are assigned to the tuple on the right of the assignment operator. The number of variables and the number of values must be equal. Otherwise it displays an error.

For example, (a,b,c,d)=(1,2,3,4)

The left side is a tuple of variables and the right side is a tuple of values. Each value is assigned to its corresponding variable. The statement performs two things:

1. Packing – place value into a new tuple
2. Unpacking – extract those values back into variables

If there are expressions on the right side all of them are evaluated before any of the assignments.

Example 2.10: Swap two values using tuple assignment

```
a=10
b=20
```

```
(a,b)=(b,a)
print(a,b)
```

Output:

```
20 10
```

2.5.3 Python Indentation

A block of code can be defined by using braces {} in most of the programming languages like C, C++ and Java. But Python uses indentation.

A block of code (body of a function, loop etc.) starts with indentation and ends with the next line without indentation.

Generally four whitespaces are used for indentation and is preferred over tabs. Here is an example.

```
for i in range(1,11):
        print(i)
if i == 5:
        break
```

2.5.4 Input, Output and Import

Python provides numerous built-in functions. Some of the functions like *input()* and *print()* are widely used for standard input and output operations respectively. Let us discuss the output section first.

a. Python output using *print()* function

print() function is used to display the output data to the standard output device (screen).

It is also possible to put the output data into a file, but this will be discussed later.

Example 2.11: ex1.py

```
print('This will be displayed the screen')
a = 5
print('The value of a is', a)
```

Output:

```
This will be displayed the screen
The value of a is 5
```

In the second *print()* statement, a space was added between the string and the value of variable ***a***. This is by default, but we can change it.

Syntax of the print() function is:

```
print(*objects, sep=' ', end='\n', file=sys.stdout, flush=False)
```

- objects are the value(s) to be printed. * indicates that there may be more than one object.

- *sep* separator is used between the values, default is a space character.
- After all values are printed, end is printed, default is a new line.
- The file is the object where the values are printed and its default value is sys.stdout (screen).

The following example illustrates this.

Example 2.12: ex2.py

```
print(1,2,3,4)
print(1,2,3,4,sep='*')
print(1,2,3,4,sep='#',end='&')
```

Output:

```
1 2 3 4
1*2*3*4
1#2#3#4&
```

Output formatting

str.*format()* method is used for formatting the output to improve clarity.

```
>>> x = 5; y = 10
>>> print('The value of x is {} and y is {}'.format(x,y))
```

Output: The value of x is 5 and y is 10

Here the curly braces {} are used as placeholders. The order in which it is printed is specified by using numbers (tuple index).

```
>>> print('I like {0} and {1}'.format('bread','butter'))
I like bread and butter

>>> print('I like {1} and {0}'.format('bread','butter'))
I like butter and bread
```

Keyword arguments can be used to format the string.

For example,

```
>>> print('Hello {name}, {greeting}'.format(greeting = 'Good Morning', name = 'Mary'))
Hello Mary, Good Morning
```

It is also possible to format the strings like the printf() function used in C programming language. % operator is used for this purpose.

```
>>> x = 98.7654321
>>> print('The value of x is %3.2f' %x)
```

```
The value of x is 98.77
>>> print('The value of x is %3.4f' %x)
The value of x is 98.7654
```

b. Python input using input() function

input() function is used to get input from the user.

The syntax for *input()* is

input([prompt])

where prompt is the string that is to be displayed on the screen. It is optional.

For Example,

```
>>> a=input("Enter number ")
Enter number 5
>>> a
'5'
```

input() function always returns a string. The user may convert the string into int or float using the function *int()* or *float()*.

For Example,

```
>>> a=float(input("Enter number "))
Enter number 4
>>> a
4.0
```

Arithmetic operations on input(string) can be performed using the *eval()* function. For Example,

```
>>> int('1+2')
Traceback (most recent call last):
File "<pyshell#16>", line 1, in <module>
int('1+2')
ValueError: invalid literal for int() with base 10: '1+2'
>>> eval('1+2')
3
```

c. Python Import

- Large programs are usually divided into different modules.
- A module is a file containing Python definitions and statements. Python modules have a filename and end with the extension .py.

- Definitions inside a module can be imported in another module or in the interactive interpreter in Python. The *import* keyword is used for this purpose.

For example, import the *math* module by typing *import* math.

```
>>> import math
>>> print(math.pi)
3.141592653589793
```

Now all the common mathematical definitions are available inside the math module. It is also possible to import some specific attributes and functions, using *from* keyword.

For example,

```
>>> from math import pi
>>> pi
3.141592653589793
```

2.6 OPERATORS

The symbols used to perform operations on the operands are called operators.

For example,

a + b

where a and b are operands, + is operator

Types of operators:

1. Arithmetic Operators
2. Relational Operators
3. Logical Operators
4. Bitwise Operators
5. Assignment Operators
6. Membership Operators
7. Identity Operators
8. Unary Arithmetic Operators

1. Arithmetic Operators

Arithmetic Operators are used to perform mathematical operations such as addition, subtraction, multiplication, division etc.

Arithmetic Operators in Python:

Table 2.5

Operator	Meaning	Example	Explanation
+	**Addition**	**a+b**	**Sum of a and b**
-	**Subtraction**	**a-b**	**Difference between a and b**
*	**Multiplication**	**a*b**	**Product of a and b**
/	**Division**	**a/b**	**Divide a by b**
//	**Quotient / Floor Division**	**a//b**	**Divide a by b and return quotient**
%	**Remainder or Modulus**	**a%b**	**Divide a by b and return remainder**
**	**Exponentiation**	**a**b**	**Return a to the power b**

Example 2.12: *example1.py*

```
a=int(input('Enter the value of a: ')) #input() function returns a string and
#it is converted to integer using int() function
b=int(input('Enter the value of b: '))
print('a + b = ', a+b) # add a and b
print('a - b = ', a-b) # subtract b from a
print('a * b = ', a*b) # multiply a and b
print('a / b = ', a/b) # divide a by b
print('a % b = ', a%b) # remainder of a by b
print('a ** b = ', a**b) # a to the power b
print('a // b = ', a//b) # quotient of a by b
```

Output:

```
Enter the value of a: 5
Enter the value of b: 3
a + b =  8
a - b =  2
a * b =  15
a / b =  1.6666666666666667
a % b =  2
a ** b =  125
a // b =  1
```

2. Relational Operators

Relational Operators are used to compare two values and return *True* or *False*. It is useful for decision making. It is also called as comparison operator.

Relational Operators in Python:

Table 2.6

Operator	Meaning	Example	Explanation
>	Greater than	a>b	True if a is greater than b
<	Less than	a<b	True if a is less than b
>=	Greater than or equal to	a>=b	True if a is greater than or equal to b
<=	Less than or equal to	a<=b	True if a is less than or equal to b
==	Equal to	a==b	True if a is equal to b
!=	Not equal to	a!=b	True if a is not equal to b

Example 2.13: ***example2.py***

```
a=int(input('Enter the value of a: '))
b=int(input('Enter the value of b: '))
print('a>b is ', a>b) # true if a>b
print('a<b is ', a<b) # true if a<b
print('a>=b is ', a>=b) # true if a>=b
print('a<=b is ', a<=b) # true if a<=b
print('a==b is ', a==b) # true if a==b
print('a!=b is ', a!=b) # true if a!=b
```

Output:

```
Enter the value of a: 12
Enter the value of b: 12
a>b is False
a<b is False
a>=b is True
a<=b is True
a==b is True
a!=b is False
```

3. Logical Operators

Logical Operators are used to combine two relational operators.

Logical Operators in Python:

Table 2.7

Operator	Meaning	Example	Explanation
And	Logical AND	a and b	True if both operands are true
Or	Logical OR	a or b	True if either of the operands is true
Not	Logical NOT	not a	True if operand is false

Example 2.14: *example3.py*

```
x=True
y=False
print('x and y is ', x and y) # true if both operands are true
print('x or y is ', x or y) # true if either of the operands is true
print('not x is ', not x) # true if operand is false
```

Output:

```
x and y is  False
x or y is  True
not x is  False
```

4. Bitwise Operators

Bitwise Operators are used to manipulate the logical operations bit by bit.

Bitwise Operators in Python:

Table 2.8

Operator	Meaning	Example	Explanation
&	Bitwise AND	a & b	True if both operands' bits are true
|	Bitwise OR	a | b	True if either of the operands' bits is true
~	Bitwise NOT	~ a	Complements the bits
^	Bitwise XOR	a^b	True if either of the operands' bits are true but not both
>>	Bitwise right shift	a>>2	Operand is shifted to right by the number of times specified
<<	Bitwise left shift	a<<2	Operand is shifted to left by the number of times specified

Truth table for bitwise operation:

Table 2.9

a	B	a&b	a|b	~a	a^b
0	0	0	0	1	0
0	1	0	1	1	1
1	0	0	1	0	1
1	1	1	1	0	0

Example 2.15:

```
>>>x=5      # x=0101
>>>y=10     # y=1010
```

```
>>>print('x&y is ',x&y)
0    #output
>>>print('x|y is ',x|y)
15   #output
>>> 10>>2 #00001010 – 2bits right shift – ans.: 00000010 i.e., 2
2    #output
>>> 10<<2 #00001010 – 2bits left shift – ans: 00101000 i.e., 40
40   #output
```

5. Assignment Operators

Assignment Operators are used in Python to assign values to variables

Table 2.10

Operator	Meaning	Example	Equivalent to
=	Equal to	x=5	x=5
+=	Plus equal to	x+=5	x=x+5
-=	Minus equal to	x-=5	x=x-5
*=	Multiplication equal to	x*=5	x=x*5
/=	Division equal to	x/=5	x=x/5
%=	Modulus equal to	x%=5	x=x%5
//=	Quotient division equal to	x//=5	x=x//5
**=	Exponent equal to	x**=5	x=x**5
&=	Bitwise AND equal to	x&=5	x=x&5
|=	Bitwise OR equal to	x|=5	x=x|5
^=	Bitwise XOR equal to	x^=5	x=x^5
>>=	Right shift equal to	x>>=2	x=x>>2
<<=	Left shift equal to	x<<=2	x=x<<2

6. Membership Operators

Membership Operators are used to test whether a value or variable is found in a sequence such as string, list, tuple, set, and dictionary. The two membership operators are *in* and *not in*.

Membership Operators in Python:

Table 2.11

Operator	Example	Explanation
in	x *in* y	True if x(value/variable) is found in the sequence y
not in	x *not in* y	True if x(value/variable) is not found in the sequence y

Example 2.16: ***example4.py***

```
x='Python Programming'
y=[1,2,3,4,5]
print('y' in x)
print('p' in x)
print('hi' in x)
print(2 in y)
print(9 in y)
```

Output

```
True
False
False
True
False
```

7. Identity Operators

Identity Operators are used to compare the memory locations of two objects. Two variables that are equal do not imply that they are identical. The two identity operators are: *is* and *is not.*

Identity Operators in Python:

Table 2.12

Operator	Example	Explanation
is	x *is* y	True if the operands x and y are identical
is not	x is *not* y	True if the operands x and y are not identical

Example 2.17: ***example5.py***

```
x1=10
y1=10
x2='Python'
y2='python'
print(x1 is y1) # integer comparison
print(x1 is not y1)
print(x2 is y2)# case sensitive, string comparison
```

Output:

```
True
False
False
```

8. Unary Operators

\+ Returns the numeric argument without any change

\- Returns the numeric argument with its sign changed

Example 2.18: example6.py

```
a=10
print(a)
c=-a
print(c)
```

Output:

```
10
-10
```

2.6.1 Precedence of Operators

If more than one operator appears in an expression, then the order of evaluation depends on the rules of precedence/priority.

Parentheses have the highest precedence. Ex.: 2 * (3-1) is 2 * 2 i.e., 4

Exponentiation has the next highest precedence. Ex.: 2**1+1 is 3, not 4

Multiplication, Division, Remainder Division and Quotient Division have the same precedence, which is higher than Addition and Subtraction, which between them have the same precedence. Ex.: 2*3-1 is 5, not 4, and 6+4/2 is 8, not 5.

Operators with the same precedence are evaluated using associativity rule i.e., either from left to right or right to left.

The following table shows the precedence and associativity of operators. The operators are listed in the decreasing order of precedence.

Table 2.13

Operators	Meaning	Associativity
()	Parentheses	Left to Right
**	Exponentiation	Right to Left
+, -, ~	Unary plus, Unary minus, Bitwise NOT	Left to Right
*, /, //, %	Multiplication, Division, Floor Division, Modulus	Left to Right
+, -	Addition, Subtraction	Left to Right
<<, >>	Bitwise shift operators	Left to Right
&	Bitwise AND	Left to Right
^, |	Bitwise XOR, Bitwise OR	Left to Right

==, !=, >, >=, <, <=	Comparisons operators	Non-associativity operators
=, %=, /=, //=, -=, +=, *=, **=	Assignment operators	
is, is not	Identity operators	Left to Right
in, not in	Membership operators	Left to Right
Not	Logical NOT	Left to Right
And	Logical AND	Left to Right
Or	Logical OR	Left to Right

Example 2.19: ***example7.py***

```
a = 20
b = 10
c = 15
d = 5
e = 0

e = (a + b) * c / d      #( 30 * 15 ) / 5
print('Value of (a + b) * c / d is ',  e)

e = ((a + b) * c) / d    # (30 * 15 ) / 5
print('Value of ((a + b) * c) / d is ',  e)

e = (a + b) * (c / d);   # (30) * (15/5)
print('Value of (a + b) * (c / d) is ',  e)

e = a + (b * c) / d;     #  20 + (150/5)
print('Value of a + (b * c) / d is ',  e)

e=d**2**3                # 5**(2**3)
print('Value of d**2**3 is ',  e)
```

Output:

```
Value of (a + b) * c / d is  90.0
Value of ((a + b) * c) / d is  90.0
Value of (a + b) * (c / d) is  90.0
Value of a + (b * c) / d is  50.0
Value of d**2**3 is  390625
```

2.7 COMMENTS

Comments are used to describe the function of a Python program. It is not executed by the interpreter. It is useful for the user to know what is going on inside the program.

If any line in the Python program starts with hash(#) symbol then it is called as comment line.

Single Line Comment:

A line starts with the # symbol.

For Example

```
# compute the percentage
percentage = (minute * 100) / 60
```

In this case, the comment appears on a separate line. Comments can be placed at the end of a line also.

Example:

```
v = 5 # assign 5 to v
```

After the # symbol it acts as comment line.

Multi-line comments

Multi line comments can be done in two ways:

1. By using hash (#) in the beginning of each line.

   For example:

   ```
   #This is a long comment
   #and it extends
   #to multiple lines
   ```

2. By using triple quotes, either ''' or """.

   For example:

   ```
   """This is also a
       perfect example of
       multi-line comments"""
   ```

Triple quotes are generally used for multi-line strings. But it can also be used for multi-line comment.

Triple quotes are used for docstrings.

a. Docstring in Python

Docstring is short for documentation string.

It is a string that is usually placed at the first statement in a module, function, class, or method definition. It tells the user what the function/class is doing.

For example:

```
>>>def double(num):
"""Function to double the value"""
```

```
return 2*num
```

Docstring can be printed on the screen by using the attribute *__doc__* of the function. The following code is used in shell to run the above program.

```
>>> print(double.__doc__)
Function to double the value
```

2.8 MODULES & FUNCTIONS

2.8.1 Definition & Use

A **module** is a file containing Python definitions and statements. The file name is the module name with the extension .py.

Within a module, the module's name (as a string) is available as the value of the global variable __name__.

For example, use the text editor to create a file called **fibo.py** in the current directory with the following contents:

Example 2.20:

```
fibo.py # Fibonacci numbers module
def fib(n): # write Fibonacci series up to n
  a,b = 0,1
  while b < n:
    print(b, end=' ')
    a,b = b,a+b
def fib2(n): # return Fibonacci series up to n
  result = []  # [] - defines a list
  a,b = 0,1
  while b < n:
    result.append(b) #append is used to insert a element into a list
    a,b = b,a+b
  return result
```

Using chevron, import this module with the following command:

```
>>> import fibo
```

Using this module name, now it is possible to access the functions:

```
>>> fibo.fib(1000)
1 1 2 3 5 8 13 21 34 55 89 144 233 377 610 987

>>> fibo.fib2(100)
[1, 1, 2, 3, 5, 8, 13, 21, 34, 55, 89]
>>> fibo.__name__
'fibo'
```

A function can assign it to a local name:

```
>>> fib = fibo.fib
>>> fib(500)
1 1 2 3 5 8 13 21 34 55 89 144 233 377
```

2.8.2 Functions

In Python, **function** is a group of related statements that perform a specific task.

- Functions can help to break a large program into smaller and modular sub-programs.
- It makes the program more organized and manageable.
- It avoids repetition and makes code reusable.

Types of functions:

1. User-defined function
2. Built-in function

User-defined function

Functions that are defined by the user according to their requirements are called **user- defined functions**. The user can modify them.

Syntax:

```
def function_name(parameters):
        """docstring"""
        statements
        return #optional
```

A function definition consists of the following components.

1. Function header that starts with the keyword *def*.
2. Function header ends with colon (:).
3. A function name which is an identifier to uniquely identify the function. Function naming follows the same rules of identifiers in Python.
4. Parameters (arguments) are used to receive the values from a function call. They are optional.
5. Optional documentation string (docstring) is used to describe what the function does.
6. One or more valid python statements make up the function body.
7. Statements must have same indentation level (usually 4 spaces).
8. An optional return statement is used to return a value from the function.

Example 2.21:

```
def greet(name):
    """This function greets the person whose name is passed in as parameter"""
    print("Hello, " + name + ". Good morning!")
```

Function Call

When a function is defined then it is possible to call it from any part of the program or from the Python prompt. A function is called by using the function name with appropriate parameters.

```
>>> greet('Paul')
Hello, Paul. Good morning!
```

The *return* statement

The *return* statement is used to exit from a function and return to the place from where it was called.

Syntax:

return (expression_list)

This statement can contain an expression which gets evaluated and the value is returned. If there is no expression in the statement or a function does not contain the *return* statement, then the function returns the *None* object.

Example 2.22:

```
>>> print(greet("Mary")) #Refer Ex. 2.21
Hello, Mary. Good morning!
None
```

Here, *None* is the returned value.

Example 2.23:

```
def mul(a,b):
  return(a*b)
def sub(a,b):
  return(a-b)
def calculate():
  a=int(input("Enter first number: "))
  b=int(input("Enter second number: "))
  result=mul(a,b)
  print(result)
  result=sub(a,b)
  print(result)
```

Output

```
>>> calculate()
Call function calculate at chevron.
Enter first number: 10
Enter second number: 20
200
-10
```

The program contains three function definitions: mul(), sub() and calculate()
The statements inside the functions do not get executed until the function is called.

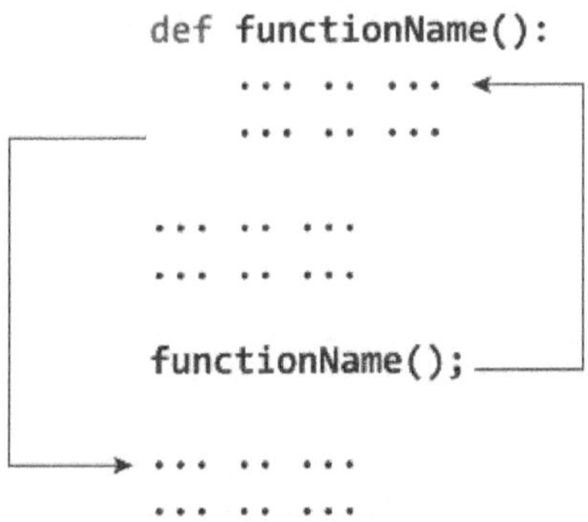

2.8.3 Flow of Execution

- The order of execution of the statements is called as the flow of execution.
- Program execution starts at the first statement of the program. Statements are executed one by one from top to bottom.
- Function definitions do not change the flow of execution of the program.
- Statements that are inside a function are not executed until the function is called.
- When a function is called the control flow jumps to the body of the function, executes all the statements inside it and then returns to the place from where the function was called.
- During the function statement execution, the function might have to execute the statements in another function. From that new function, the program might have to execute yet another function!
- A function completes its execution then returns to the place in the function that called. When it gets to the end of the program, it terminates.

Built-in Functions

Built-in Functions are already predefined in Python interpreter and are readily available for use.

For Example,

print() – used to display the information into the screen
input() used to get the input from the user. It is always in string
abs() – used to return the absolute value of a number
len() – used to return the length of a string
ord() – used to return a ASCII value of a character.

Example: To find ASCII value of given character

```
c=input("Enter a character: ")
print("ASCII value of "+c+" is: ",ord(c))
```

Output:

```
Enter a character: p
ASCII value of p is:  112
```

Type conversion functions:

Python provides built-in functions that convert values from one type to another.

Function Name	Description	Example

int()	Convert a string or float into an integer	>>> int('2020')
		2020
		>>> int(3.14)
		3

float()	Convert a string or integer into float	>>> float('2.1')
		2.1
		>>> float(4)
		4.0

str()	Convert a integer, float, list, tuple or dictionary into string	>>> str(3.14)
		'3.14'
		>>> str([10,20,30,40])
		'[10, 20, 30, 40]'

list()	Convert a string , tuple or dictionary into list	>>> list('Mary')
		['M', 'a', 'r', 'y']
		>>> list((10,20,30,40))
		[10, 20, 30, 40]

tuple()	Convert a string or tuple into list	>>> tuple('Mary') ('M', 'a', 'r', 'y') >>> tuple([10,20,30,40]) (10, 20, 30, 40)

Math Functions:

Math module is used to support the mathematical functions in Python. A module is a file that contains a collection of related functions. Before using mathematical built-in functions, import math module.

```
>>> import math
```

It will create a module object named math which contains functions and variables defined in the module. The math functions in the module include the following:

Function Name	Description	Example
abs(n)	Returns the absolute value of a number n	>>> abs(-8) 8
round(n,d)	Rounds a number(n) to a number of decimal points(d)	>>> round(3.1415,2) 3.14
floor(n)	Rounds down to the nearest integer	>>> math.floor(5.6) 5
ceil(n)	Rounds up to the nearest integer	>>> math.ceil(5.6) 6
pow(n,d)	Returns n^d value	>>> math.pow(3,4) 81.0
sqrt(n)	Returns the square root of a number n	>>> math.sqrt(81) 9.0
factorial(n)	Returns the factorial value of n	>>> math.factorial(4) 24
gcd(n,m)	Returns the greatest common divisor	>>> math.gcd(25,125) 25
trunc(x)	Returns the integer value of x and truncates the fraction	>>> math.trunc(2.78) 2

Mathematical constants:

math.pi–returns the mathematical constant value π(3.141592)

math.e-returns the mathematical constant value e(2.718281)

2.8.4 Parameters and Arguments

A variable inside a function header is called as **parameter**. A value that is assigned to the parameter through a function call is called **argument**.

When a function is called, the arguments are assigned to the function header variables called parameters. For example, a user-defined function that takes an argument and prints it twice is shown below:

```
def print_twice(num):
        print(num)
        print(num)
```

When the function print_twice() is called, the argument is assigned to a function definition parameter named ***num***. Then, it prints the value of the parameter ***num*** twice.

```
>>> print_twice(20)
20
20
>>> print_twice(math.pi)
3.14159265359
3.14159265359
```

The same rules of composition that apply to built-in functions also apply to user-defined functions; so, the user can use any kind of expression as an argument for print_twice:

```
>>> print_twice('ab '*3)
ab ab ab
ab ab ab
>>> import math
>>> print_twice(math.cos(math.pi))
-1.0
-1.0
```

The argument is evaluated before the function is called. In this example the expressions 'ab '*3 and *math.cos(math.pi)* are evaluated first.

It is also possible to use a variable as an argument:

```
>>> a = 'Welcome'
>>> print_twice(a)
Welcome
Welcome
```

The variable ***a*** is passed as an argument from the function call and it is assigned to the parameter ***num*** in the function definition.

Variables and parameters are local

If a variable is created inside a function then it is called as local variable. It means that the life time of the local variable exists only inside the function. For example:

```
def add(a,b):
        c=a+b
        print_twice(c)
```

This function takes two arguments. If the arguments are integers then it directly performs the addition, and prints the result twice. If the arguments are strings then it concatenates them, and prints the result twice. For example:

```
>>> a=10
>>> b=20
>>> add(a,b)
30
30
>>> a='Hi'
>>> b=' Welcome'
>>> add(a,b)
Hi Welcome
Hi Welcome
```

When the function add() terminates, the variable ***c*** is destroyed. Now trying to print ***c*** will get an error.

```
>>> print(c)
Trace back (most recent call last):
File "<pyshell#18>", line 1, in <module>
print(c)
Name Error: name 'c' is not defined
```

2.8.5 Fruitful functions and void functions

Fruitful functions are functions that return one or more values. If a fruitful function is called it gives a result. Some user-defined functions may not return any value. They are called void functions.

When a fruitful function is called, the programmer almost always wants to do something with the result;

For example, the result is assigned to a variable or used as a part of an expression:

```
>>> x=math.cos(30)
```

```
>>> print(x)
0.15425144988758405
>>> x=x+5
>>> print(x)
5.154251449887584
```

When a fruitful function is called in interactive mode, Python displays the result; for example:

```
>>> math.sqrt(5)
2.2360679774997898
```

Void functions might display something on the screen or have some other effect, but they do not have a return value. If you try to assign the result to a variable, you get a special value called *None*.

```
>>> result = print_twice('ab')
ab
ab
>>> print result
None
```

The value *None* is not the same as the string 'None'. It is a special value that has its own type:

```
>>> print type(None)
<type 'NoneType'>
```

2.9 ILLUSTRATIVE PROGRAMS

2.9.1 Write a Python program to exchange the value of two variables

Ans:

Program:

```
# take input from the user
x = int(input('Enter the value of x: '))
y = int(input('Enter the value of y: '))
# create a temporary variable and swap the values
temp = x
x = y
y = temp
print('The value of x after swapping: {}'.format(x))
print('The value of y after swapping: {}'.format(y))
```

Output:

```
Enter the value of x: 20
Enter the value of y: 10
The value of x after swapping: 10
The value of y after swapping: 20
```

2.9.2 Write a Python Program to find the distance between two points

Ans:

Program:

```
import math
x1=int(input("Enter the value of x1: "))
x2=int(input("Enter the value of x2: "))
y1=int(input("Enter the value of y1: "))
y2=int(input("Enter the value of y2: "))
distance=math.sqrt(((x1-y1)**2)+((x2-y2)**2))
print("Distance between two points:%d"%distance)
```

Output:

```
Enter the value of x1: 2
Enter the value of x2: 4
Enter the value of y1: 3
Enter the value of y2: 6
Distance between two points:2
```

2.9.3 Write a Python program to circulate the values of n variables

Ans:

(The above problem can be easily solved in Python using list as below. Unit IV discusses 'list' in detail.)

Program:

```
def rotate(list,n):
    new=list[n:]+list[:n]
    return new
    example=[1,2,3,4,5]
    print("Original list:",example)
    a=rotate(example,1)
    print("List rotated clockwise by 1 position:",a)
    a=rotate(example,2)
    print("List rotated clockwise by 1 position:",a)
    a=rotate(example,-2)
    print("List rotated clockwise by 1 position:",a)
```

Output:

```
Original list: [1, 2, 3, 4, 5]
List rotated clockwise by 1: [2, 3, 4, 5, 1]
List rotated clockwise by 1: [3, 4, 5, 1, 2]
List rotated clockwise by 1: [4, 5, 1, 2, 3]
```

Short Questions

1. What is meant by interpreter?

Interpreter is used to convert the source code into machine language line by line. The interpreter provides an interactive environment with the Python programming language. There are two ways to use the interpreter:

1. **Interactive mode**

   In **interactive mode**, the program statements can be typed in the prompt and the interpreter displays the result instantly. For example:

```
>>>1+1
```

Output:

```
2
```

The prompt >>> (chevron) indicates that the interpreter is ready. This interactive mode execution is convenient for smaller programs.

2. **Script mode**

   In **script mode**, the program can be stored in a file (eg: Notepad) and the interpreter can be used to execute the file. The python script's filename ends with **.py** extension. For larger programs, the program code can be stored as a script and executed in the future.

   For example, the following script may be stored as add.py

```
# Add two numbers
a=2
b=3
c=a+b
print(c)
```

Output: 5

2. How will you invoke the python interpreter?

The Python interpreter can be invoked by typing the command "python" without any parameter followed by the "return" key at the shell prompt.

3. What is meant by interactive mode of the interpreter?

Interactive mode is a command line shell which gives immediate feedback for each statement, with previously fed statements in active memory.

```
>>>1+1
2
```

The prompt >>> (chevron) indicates that the interpreter is ready. This interactive mode execution is convenient for smaller programs.

4. Write a snippet to display "Hello World" in python interpreter.

(Snippet refers to a small part of a program)

In script mode:

```
>>> print ("HelloWorld" )
Hello World
```

In Interactive Mode:

```
>>>"Hello World"
'Hello World'
```

5. What is a value? What are the different types of values?

Value is one of the basic things with which a program works, like a letter or a number that a program manipulates. Its types are: integer, float, boolean, strings and lists.

Example:

1, 2 (integer)

'Hello! World' (String)

6. Define a variable and write down the rules for naming a variable.

A name that refers to a value is a variable. A variable is a location in memory used to store some data (value). Variable names can be arbitrarily long. They can contain both letters and numbers, but they have to begin with a letter. Keywords cannot be used as variable name.

7. Define keyword and enumerate some of the keywords in Python.

A keyword is a reserved word that is used by the compiler (or interpreter) for a specific operations or purpose in a program. Keywords cannot be used as variable names. Some of the keywords used in python are: *and, del, from, not, while, is, continue*.

8. Define statement. What are its types?

Instructions that a Python interpreter can execute are called **statements**. For example, a=1 is an assignment statement. A statement is a unit of code that the interpreter executes. Types are: assignment statement, print statement, control statement, looping statement.

For Example

```
x=2 # assignment statement
print x #print statement
```

Output:

```
2
```

9. What do you mean by an assignment statement?

An assignment statement creates new variables and gives them values:

Ex. 1: Message = 'Welcome' #Message is a variable and 'Welcome' is its value

Ex. 2: n = 17 #n is a variable and 17 is its value

10. What is tuple assignment? (AU, *Jan 2018)*

Python allows a tuple of variables on the left of an assignment operator and values to be assigned to the tuple on the right of the assignment operator. The number of variables and the number of values must be equal. Otherwise it displays an error.

For example, (a,b,c,d)=(1,2,3,4)

11. What is an expression?

An **expression** is a combination of operands and operators.

Example:

```
>>>x=10
>>>x + 17
```

12. What do you mean by an operand and an operator? Illustrate your answer with relevant example.

The symbols used to perform operations on the operands are called operators. The data items that an operator acts upon are called operands.

For example,

a + b

where a and b are operands, and + is operator.

There are different operators like Arithmetic, Relational, Logical, etc.

13. What is the order in which operations are evaluated? Give the order of precedence.

If more than one operator appears in an expression, then the order of evaluation depends on the rules of precedence/priority.

1. Parentheses have the highest precedence. Ex. 2 * (3-1) is 2 * 2 i.e., 4
2. Exponentiation has the next highest precedence. Ex. 2**1+1 is 3, not 4
3. Multiplication, Division, Remainder Division and Quotient Division have the same precedence, which is higher than Addition and Subtraction, which have the same precedence between them. Ex. 2*3-1 is 5, not 4, and 6+4/2 is 8, not 5.

4. When more than one operator with same precedence appears in an expression then the left to right order is followed.

14. Illustrate the use of * and + operators in strings with example.

The * operator performs repetition on strings and the + operator performs concatenation on strings.

Example:

```
>>> 'Hello'*3
```

Output: 'HelloHelloHello'

```
>>> 'Hello'+'World'
```

Output: 'HelloWorld'

15. What is the symbol for comment? Give an example.

is the symbol for comments in Python.

Example:

```
# this statement computes the average
```

16. What is function call?

When a function is defined then it is possible to call it from any part of a program or from the Python prompt. A function is called by using the function name with appropriate arguments.

Ex.: #Greet Function definition

```
def greet(name):
   """This function greets
 the person whose name is passed in as parameter"""
   print("Hello, " + name + ". Good morning!")
greet ('Paul') #Function call
```

Output

```
Hello, Paul. Good morning!
```

17. Identify the parts of a function in the given example.

>>> betty = type("32")

>>> print(betty)

type is predefined function, and it displays the type of a value or variable. The value or variable, which is called the argument of the function, is enclosed in parentheses. The argument is "32". The function returns the result called return value. The return value is stored in *betty*.

18. What is a local variable?

A variable defined inside a function is called local variable. A local variable can only be used inside the function in which it is defined.

19. What is the output of the following?

a. float(32)

b. float("3.14159")

Output:

a. 32.0 # the float function converts integers to floating-point numbers.

b. 3.14159 # the float function converts strings to floating-point numbers.

20. What do you mean by flow of execution?

- The order of execution of the statements is called as the flow of execution.
- Program execution starts at the first statement of the program. Statements are executed one by one from top to bottom.
- Function definitions do not change the flow of execution of the program.
- Statements that are inside a function are not executed until the function is called.

21. Write down the output for the following program.

```
first='hello'
second='world'
print(first + second)
```

Output:

helloworld

22. Write the syntax of function definition.

```
def function_name(list of parameters):
        statements
```

23. Explain the concept of floor (or quotient) division.

The operation that divides two numbers and truncates the fraction part is known as floor division. The symbol for this division in Python is '//'. For example, 4//3 is 1.

24. What is type coercion? Give example.

Automatic method to convert between numeric data types is called type coercion. For mathematical operators, if any one operand is a float, the other is automatically converted to float.

Eg:

```
>>> minute = 59
>>> minute / 60.0
```

Output: 0.983333333333

25. Write a math function to perform √2 / 2.

```
>>> math.sqrt(2) / 2.0
```

Output: 0.707106781187

26. What is meant by traceback?

A **traceback** is a report containing the function calls made in the code at a specific point. Whenever the code gets an exception, the **traceback** will give the information about what went wrong in the code.

A traceback tells us the name of the program file in which the error occurred, and what line, and what functions were executing at the time. It also shows the line of code that caused the error and specifies the name of the error.

For example, **sample.py**

```
profit=1000
print('$'+profit)
```

Output:

```
Traceback (most recent call last):
  File "C:/Python/Python37-32/sample.py", line 2, in <module>
    print('$'+profit)
TypeError: can only concatenate str (not "int") to str
```

27. Name the four types of scalar objects Python has. *(AU, Jan 2018)*

Scalar is a type that can have a single value such as 4, 2.13, 'Alice'.

Four types are: int, float, complex, bool and str

Unsolved Exercises

1. Assume that the following assignment statement has been executed:

   width, height, delimiter = 21,14, ', '

   For each of the following expressions, find the value of the expression and the type. Use the Python interpreter to check the answers.

   i) width/4
   ii) width/4.0
   iii) 3+2**3
   iv) delimiter*3

2. Find the volume of a sphere with radius 5 using Python interpreter.
3. Find the data type of the data given below using *type()* function:

   i) 'hello'
   ii) -234
   iii) 53.j
   iv) 2.34e10

4. Evaluate the following expressions:

   i) 20>15 and 12<15 or 10<=23
   ii) 5**3==125 and 7!=8

iii) 10!=10 and not(7<3)

iv) 5*2==10 and not(7<3)

5. Write a Python program to compute the area of parallelogram and Trapezoid.
6. Write a Python program to find the volume of Cone and Cube.
7. Write a Python program to compute x^y
8. Write a Python program to calculate simple interest and compound interest.
9. Evaluate the following expressions:

i) 5**3+11//2

ii) 10/2+20-15*2

iii) 21%4*4+10-3**3

10. Find the value of the following expressions if x=5, y=3 and z=1

i) x==y or y>z

ii) x!=y and z<y

iii) x**3-y//2+z

UNIT III
CONTROL FLOW, FUNCTIONS

Contents

Conditionals: Boolean values and operators, conditional (if), alternative (if-else), chained conditional (if-elif-else); Iteration: state, while, for, break, continue, pass; Fruitful functions: return values, parameters, scope: local and global, composition, recursion; Strings: string slices, immutability, string functions and methods, string module; Lists as arrays. Illustrative programs: square root, gcd, exponentiation, sum the array of numbers, linear search, binary search.

3.1 CONDITIONALS

3.1.1 Boolean Values

Boolean values are *True* (1) and *False* (0). Non-zero values are *True*. The following values are considered false:

- None
- *False*
- zero of any numeric type, for example, 0, 0L, 0.0, 0j.
- any empty sequence, for example, '', (), [].
- any empty mapping, for example, {}.

All other values are considered true.

Operations and built-in functions that have a Boolean result always return 0 or *False* for false and 1 or *True* for true, unless otherwise stated.

The relational operators such as ==, !=, <, <=, >, >= and the logical operators such as *and, or, not* are the Boolean operators. The statement that results in either *True* or *False* is a Boolean expression.

3.1.2 Operators

-Refer Unit II.-

Example 3.1: Using relational operators

```
x=5
y=8
print(str(x)+'>'+str(y)+' is ',x>y)
print(str(x)+'<'+str(y)+' is ',x<y)
print(str(x)+'=='+str(y)+' is ',x==y)
print(str(x)+'!='+str(y)+' is ',x!=y)
print(str(x)+'>='+str(y)+' is ',x>=y)
print(str(x)+'<='+str(y)+' is ',x<=y)
```

Output:

```
5>8 is  False
5<8 is  True
5==8 is  False
5!=8 is  True
5>=8 is  False
5<=8 is  True
```

Example 3.2: Using logical operators

```
x=True
y=False
print(str(x)+' and '+str(y)+' is ',x and y)
print(str(x)+' or '+str(y)+' is ',x or y)
print('not '+str(x)+' is ',not x)
```

Output:

```
True and False is  False
True or False is  True
not True is  False
```

3.1.3 Conditional Statements

1. *if* statement
2. *if-else* statement / Alternative
3. *if-elif-else* statement / Chained conditional
4. Nested *if* conditional statement

1. *if* statement

Used to check a condition and control the flow of execution

Syntax:

```
if condition:
        block of statements
```

Flowchart:

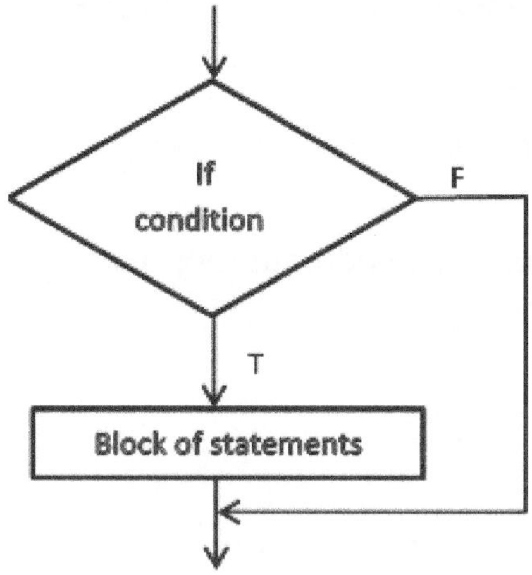

Fig 3.1

Example 3.3:

```
number=10
if number>0:
  print(number," is a positive number")
number=-1
if number>0:
  print(number," is a positive number")
```

Output:

```
10 is a positive number
```

2. *if-else* statement / Alternative

If the condition is true then it will execute the true block statements otherwise it will execute false block statements.

Syntax:

if condition:
    true block statements
else:
    false block statements

Flowchart:

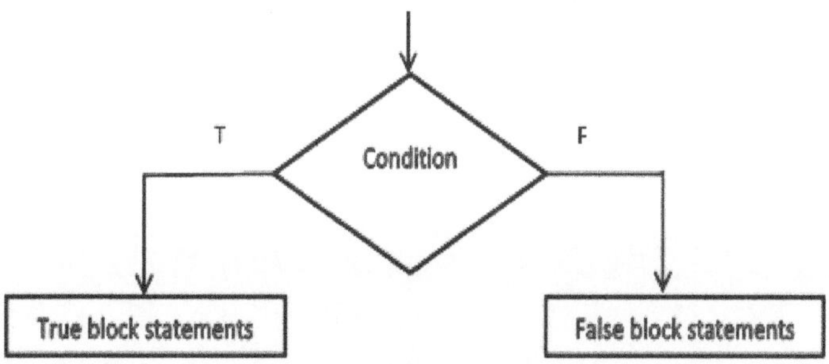

Fig 3.2

Example 3.4:

```
number=28
if number%2==0:
   print(number," is an even number")
else:
   print(number," is an odd number")
```

Output:

```
28 is an even number
```

3. *if-elif-else* statement / Chained Condition

It is used to test more than one condition.

elif is short form for else-if. It is a multipath decision statement. It is used to check multiple conditions. The conditions are executed from the top to the bottom. If the condition 1 is false it checks the condition 2 of the next *elif* block and so on.

If all the conditions are false then the else statement is executed. *if-elif* contains one *else* block. But it can have multiple *elif* blocks.

Syntax:

```
if condition 1:
        statements
elif condition 2:
        statements
.
.
.
elif condition n:
        statements
else:
        statements
```

Flowchart

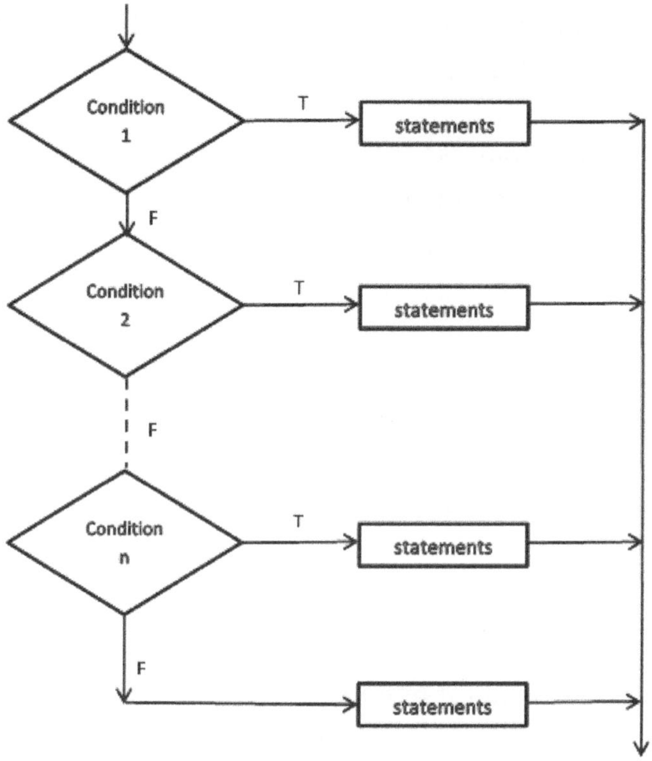

Fig 3.3

Example 3.5:

```
a=float(input("Enter the number: "))
if a>0:
  print("The given number is a positive number")
elif a==0:
  print("The given number is Zero")
else:
  print("The given number is a negative number")
```

Output:

```
Enter the number: -4
The given number is negative number
>>>
Enter the number: 10
The given number is a positive number
>>>
Enter the number: 0
The given number is Zero
```

4. Nested if statement

If an *if* statement contains another *if* statement it is called as 'nested if' statement. Indentations must be clear in the flow of statements.

Example 3.6: Find the smallest of three numbers

```
a=int(input("Enter the value of a: "))
b=int(input("Enter the value of b: "))
c=int(input("Enter the value of c: "))
if a<b:
    if a<c:
        print('The smallest number is ',a)
    else:
        print('The smallest number is ',c)
elif b<c:
    print('The smallest number is ',b)
else:
    print('The smallest number is ',c)
```

Output:

```
Enter the value of a: 5
Enter the value of b: 2
Enter the value of c: 7
The smallest number is 2
```

3.2 ITERATION

When a set of statements is executed repeatedly until a specified condition becomes true it is called as iteration.

Types:

1. *while*
2. *for*

State

State is a behavioural design pattern that allows an object to change the behaviour when its internal state changes.

3.2.1 *while* loop (Entry-controlled loop)

It is an entry-controlled loop

It executes a block of statements repeatedly until the condition becomes False.

Syntax:

```
while condition:
        block of statements
next statement
```

Flowchart:

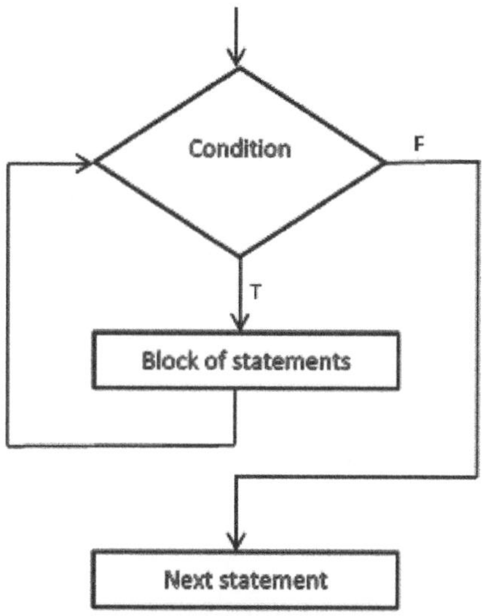

Fig 3.4

Example 3.7:

```
count=0
while count<5:
  print("The count value is",count)
  count=count+1
```

Output:

```
The count value is 0
The count value is 1
The count value is 2
The count value is 3
The count value is 4
```

Steps involved in *while* loop:

1. Check the *while* condition first.
2. If the condition is true then it will execute the block of statements in *while* loop.
3. If the condition is false then it will exit from the *while* loop and continue the execution at the next statement.

***while* loop with *else* statement:**

An optional *else* block is available in *while* loop. The *else* block is executed if the *while* condition is false.

The *while* loop can be terminated with a *break* statement, in such case *else* block is not executed.

Syntax:

```
while condition:
        block of statements
else:
        else block statement
```

Example 3.8:

```
count=0
while count<5:
  print("The count value is",count)
  count=count+1
else:
  print("Exit")
```

Output:

```
The count value is 0
The count value is 1
The count value is 2
The count value is 3
The count value is 4
Exit
```

3.2.2 Nested *while*

When a *while* loop is placed inside another *while* loop it is called 'nested *while*' loop.

Syntax:

```
while condition:
        while condition:
                statements
```

Example 3.9:

```
x=-2
y=2
while x<=y:
  print("x =",x)
  x=x+1
```

```
while(x<=0):
  print("x is negative")
  x=x+1
```

Output:

```
x = -2
x is negative
x is negative
x = 1
x = 2
```

3.2.3 *for* loop

***for* loop** is used to execute a sequence of statements multiple times. If the number of times 'n' a set statements is to be executed is already known then *for* loop is chosen.

Syntax:

```
for val in sequence:
        statements
```

- 'val' is a variable that takes value of the item inside the sequence on each iteration.
- Loop continues until the last item in the sequence is reached.
- *for* loop contains initialization & condition part, but increment and decrement need not be defined in Python.

Advantages

Highly Flexible

More concise and easy to use

Example 3.10:

```
word = "hello"
for letter in word:
  print(letter)
```

Output:

```
h
e
l
l
o
```

In this example, ***word*** variable contains the string "hello". Using *for* loop, each character in ***word*** sequence is assigned to the variable ***letter*** and it is displayed. This process is repeated until it reaches the end of the string.

Example 3.11:

```
num=[20,30,40]
for i in num:
  print("The value of i is",i)
```

Output:

```
The value of i is 20
The value of i is 30
The value of i is 40
```

In this example, **num** variable is a list containing three integer values. Using *for* loop, each value in **num** sequence is assigned to the variable **i** and it is displayed. This process is repeated until it reaches the end of the list.

3.2.4 range()

range() is a built-in function. It is used for iteration in *for* loop.

Default initial value of *range()* is 0.

Syntax:

range([start],stop,[step])

where, start is the starting number of the sequence(optional, default is 0)

stop is end value i.e., stop-1

step is difference between each number in that sequence(optional, default is 1).

Example 3.12:

```
print("Range with one argument")
for i in range(5): #start at 0 end before 5 in steps of 1
  print(i)
print("Range with two arguments")
for i in range(10,20): #start at 10 end before 20 insteps of 1
  print(i)
print("Range with three arguments")
for i in range(50,70,3):  #start at 50 end before 70 in steps of 3
  print(i)
```

Output:

```
Range with one argument
0
1
2
```

```
3
4
Range with two arguments
10
11
12
13
14
15
16
17
18
19
Range with three arguments
50
53
56
59
62
65
68
```

3.2.5 xrange()

xrange() function works similar to *range()* but returns a xrange object.

It works only in Python 2nd version.

It uses less memory.

Syntax:

```
xrange([start],stop,[step])
```

Example 3.13:

```
print("xrange with single argument")
for i in xrange(6):
  print(i)
print("xrange with two arguments")
for i in xrange(1,7):
  print(i)
print("xrange with three arguments")
for i in xrange(1,10,3):
  print(i)
```

Output:

```
xrange with single argument
0
1
2
3
4
5
xrange with two arguments
1
2
3
4
5
6
xrange with three arguments
1
4
7
```

Differences between range() and xrange():

Table 3.1

range()	xrange()
1. range() function returns a range object	1. xrange() function returns a xrange object
2. It takes more memory because the return type of range() is list.	2. It takes less memory because the variable stores only the range and return type of xrange() is xrange object.
3. range() returns the list. All the operations that can be applied on list can be used on it.	3. xrange() returns a xrange object. Operations associated to list cannot be applied on them.
4. Slower implementation	4. Faster implementation

3.2.6 *for* loop with *else* statement:

An optional *else* block is available in *for* loop. The *else* block is executed if the items in the sequence used in *for* loop are exhausted.

break statement can be used to stop a *for* loop.

In such a case, the *else* part is ignored.

Syntax:

```
for val in sequence:
        block of statements
else:
        else block statement
```

Example 3.14:

```
num=[10,20,30,40]
for i in num:
  print("The value of i is",i)
else:
  print("Exit")
```

Output:

```
The value of i is 10
The value of i is 20
The value of i is 30
The value of i is 40
Exit
```

3.2.7 Nested for loops

If a *for* loop contains another *for* loop, it is called as nested *for* loop.

Syntax:

```
for val in sequence:
        for val in sequence:
                statements
```

Example 3.15:

```
for x in range(1,3):
  for y in range(1,5):
    print(x,"*",y,"=",x*y)
```

Output:

```
1 * 1 = 1
1 * 2 = 2
```

1 * 3 = 3
1 * 4 = 4
2 * 1 = 2
2 * 2 = 4
2 * 3 = 6
2 * 4 = 8

3.3 LOOP CONTROL STATEMENTS

Loop control statements are used to change the execution from its normal sequence. Python supports three loop control statements.

1. *break*
2. *continue*
3. *pass*

3.3.1 *break* statement

break statement is used to bring the control out of the loop. It terminates the loop statement and transfers execution to the statement immediately following the loop.

Syntax:

break

Flowchart

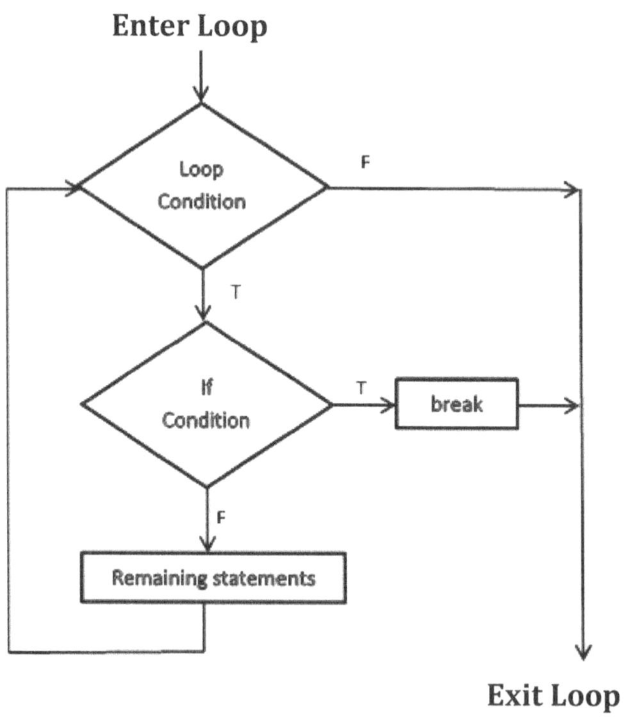

Fig. 3.5

Example 3.16:

```
for x in range(1,10):
   if x==5:
      break
   print("x=",x)
```

Output:

```
x= 1
x= 2
x= 3
x= 4
```

If x=5, it exits from *for* loop.

3.3.2 *continue* statement

continue statement is used to return the control to the beginning of the loop. It skips all remaining statements in the current iteration of the loop and moves the control back to the top of the loop. It can be used both in *while* and *for* loops.

Syntax:

continue

Flowchart

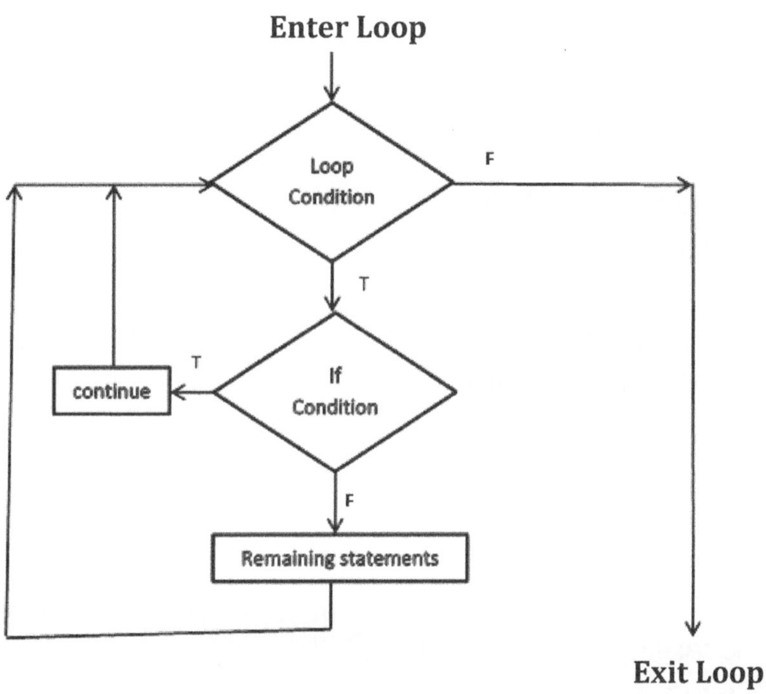

Fig. 3.6

Example 3.17:

```
for x in range(1,10):
  if x==5:
    continue
  print("x=",x)
```

Output:

```
x= 1
x= 2
x= 3
x= 4
x= 6
x= 7
x= 8
x= 9
```

3.3.3 *pass* statement

The *pass* statement in Python is used when a statement is required syntactically but you do not want any command or code to execute.

The pass statement is a null operation; nothing happens when it executes.

Syntax:

pass

Example 3.18:

```
for letter in "python":
  if letter=="h":
    pass
    print("pass block")
  print("letter=",letter)
```

Output:

```
letter= p
letter= y
letter= t
pass block
letter= h
letter= o
letter= n
```

3.4 FRUITFUL FUNCTIONS

Fruitful functions are functions that return values. Its result is returned to the caller as the "fruit" of called function. It may be built-in or user-defined functions.

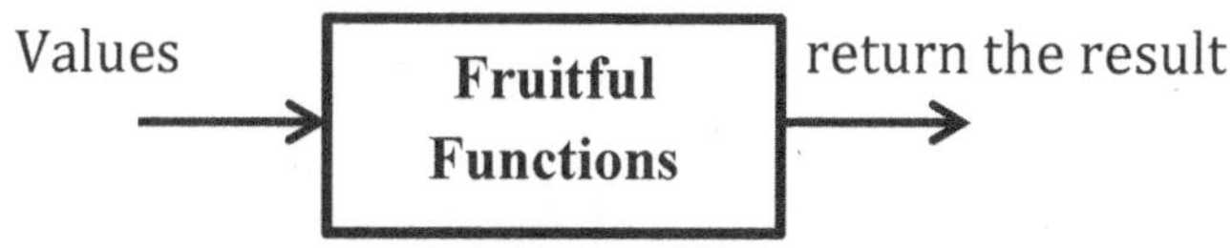

Fig. 3.7

Example 3.19:

```
def square(b):
  c=b*b
  return c
b=int(input("Enter the b value: "))
result=square(b)
print("The square of ",b," is ",result)
```

Output:

```
Enter the b value: 7
The square of 7 is 49
```

Void Function

If the function definition does not return any value then it is called as void function.

Example 3.20:

```
def square(b):
  c=b*b
  print("The square of ",b," is ",c)
b=int(input("Enter the b value: "))
square(b)
```

Output:

```
Enter the b value: 5
The square of  5  is  25
```

3.4.1 *Return* values

return is a keyword which is used to return a value from the function definition block to the calling function.

return takes zero, values or an expression.

Default value is *None.*

If more than one value has to be returned then a tuple or list is used.

Syntax:

return

or

return expression

Example: Refer Example 3.19

Dead Code

Statements that appear after a *return* statement in a function or any other place that the flow of execution can never reach is called as **dead code**.

3.4.2 Arguments

From the function call, the inputs are given to a function definition. These inputs are called as **arguments.**

Types:

1. Required arguments.
2. Keyword arguments.
3. Default arguments.
4. Variable-length arguments.

1. Required argument

The argument that must be present in a function call matching the corresponding parameter in the called function is called required argument. With **required arguments**, the number of arguments in the function call should exactly match with the parameters in the function definition. If the arguments do not match with the parameters then it results in an error.

Example 3.21:

```
def display(s):
  print(s)
  return
display(100)
display(100,5)
```

Output:

```
100
TypeError: display() takes 1 positional argument but 2 were given
```

2. Keyword argument

With **keyword argument**, the called function identifies the arguments by the parameter name. It is possible to skip the arguments or place the arguments out of order in the function call. Python interpreter uses the 'keyword' to match the values with parameters.

Function using keyword arguments takes the form: keyword=value

Example 3.22:

```
def display(s,d):
    print(s,d)
    return
display(s=500,d="Green")
display(d="Green",s=500)
```

Output:

```
500 Green
500 Green
```

3. Default argument

Default argument assumes the default value given in the function definition, if a value is not provided in function call for that argument.

Example 3.23:

```
def display(s,d=20): #default value is 20 for d
    print(d,s)
    return
display(50)
display(50,15)
```

Output:

```
20 50
15 50
```

4. Variable-length argument

Sometimes, the number of arguments that are passed to a function is not known in advance. Python allows handling this situation through function call with arbitrary number of arguments or variable length argument.

An asterisk (*) is used before the parameter name to denote this kind of argument.

Example 3.24:

```
def display(*s): #Number of arguments given in the call for parameter 's'
#may vary
    for i in s:
        print(i)
    return
display(1,2,3)
display("Hi")
```

Output:

```
1
2
3
Hi
```

Example 3.25: #Program to add two numbers by passing parameters

```
def add(a,b):
    c=a+b
    return c
x=int(input("Enter the value of x: "))
y=int(input("Enter the value of y: "))
z=add(x,y)
print(z)
```

Output:

```
Enter the value of x: 4
Enter the value of y: 6
10
```

3.4.3 Parameters

In fruitful function, two types of parameters are used:

1. Formal parameters
2. Actual parameters

Arguments that are used in a function call are called as actual parameters.

Parameters that are used in function definition is called as formal parameters.

Example 3.26:

```
def cube(x): # 'x' is a formal parameter
    return x*x*x
```

```
a=int(input("Enter the value of a: "))
b=cube(a) # 'a' is an actual parameter
print("Cube of the given number ",b)
```

Output:

```
Enter the value of a: 3
Cube of the given number 27
```

3.4.4 Scope and lifetime of Variables

In a program, the part in which a variable is accessible is called its scope, and how long the variable exists is called its lifetime.

Based on the scope the variables are classified as:

1. Global variables
2. Local variables

A variable defined in the main body of a program is called as a global variable. It is visible throughout the program.

A variable defined inside a function is called as a local variable to that function. It is visible only inside that function.

Example 3.27:

```
def display(a):
  a=10
  print("Value inside function:",a)
  return a
a=20
print("Value when return is used:",display(a))
print("Value outside function:",a)
```

Output:

```
Value inside function: 10
Value when return is used: 10
Value outside function: 20
```

3.4.5 Composition

The ability of calling one function from within another function is called as composition. It is a way of combining functions such that the result of called function is passed as the argument of the calling function.

Example 3.28: #Program to find square of a number

```
c=float(input("Enter a value: "))
```

```
d=c**2
print(d)
```

Output:

```
Enter a value: 3
9.0
```

- Here the *input* function is used inside *float* function; it is called as composition.
- *input* function always produces the result as a string. Based on the requirement it is converted to either *int()* or *float()*.

3.4.6 Recursion

A function called by itself is called as a recursive function. Recursion is a process of calling a function by itself again and again until some condition is satisfied.

A recursive function must have

1. A statement to test whether the function is calling itself again.
2. A statement that calls the function itself with an argument.
3. A conditional statement to make the exit from recursion possible
4. A *return* statement.

Example 3.29: #Program to find factorial using recursion

```
def factorial(n):
  if n==1:
    return 1
  else:
    return n*factorial(n-1)
print(factorial(5))
```

Output:

```
120
```

Example 3.30: #Program to find the Fibonacci Series till 10 terms

```
def fibo(n):
  if n<=1:
    return n
  else:
    return(fibo(n-1)+fibo(n-2))
terms=10
print("Fibonacci Series")
```

```
for i in range(terms):
   print(fibo(i))
```

Output:

```
Fibonacci Series
0
1
1
2
3
5
8
13
21
34
```

Advantages of recursion:

1. The code looks clean and elegant.
2. Complex tasks are divided into simpler sub-problems
3. Sequence generation is easier with recursion

Disadvantages of recursion:

1. Logic is difficult to follow.
2. It takes more memory.
3. It is hard to debug.

3.5 STRINGS

String is a sequence of characters enclosed within single quotes (' '), double quotes (" "), triple single quotes (''' ''') or triple double quotes(""" """).

- Characters may be a alphabet or digit or any special characters.
- Strings are immutable i.e., characters can be accessed but it is not possible to change.
- An empty string is a string that has no characters.
- Single quote is used to represent a word.
- Double quote is used to represent a single sentence.
- Triple quote is used to represent a multiline string.

Each string is stored in the computer's memory as a list of characters. Each character is accessed using its index. There are two types of indexing.

1. Positive Indexing

   String characters are referred from left to right by using 0, 1, 2, ...

2. Negative Indexing

String characters are referred from right to left by using -1, -2, -3, ...

For example,

str='WELCOME'

0	1	2	3	4	5	6
W	E	L	C	O	M	E
-7	-6	-5	-4	-3	-2	-1

Example 3.31:

```
s='Word'
print(s)
s="This is a sentence"
print(s)
s='''This is a paragraph. It is made up of multiple words, multiple lines
and multiple sentences'''
print(s)
s=' '
print(s)
s="""Single quote is used to represent a word. Double quote is used to
represent a single sentence. Triple quote is used to represent a multiline
string. """
print(s)
```

Output:

```
Word
This is a sentence
This is a paragraph. It is made up of multiple words, multiple lines and
multiple sentences

Single quote is used to represent a word. Double quote is used to
represent a single sentence. Triple quote is used to represent a
multiline string.
```

3.5.1 String Slices

A part of a string is called as slice.

Slice is used to take sub parts of either a list or a string. [] is used as a slice operator.

Syntax:

Substring=originalstring[m:n]

m - Starting index which is to be included

n - Ending index which is to be excluded

- If the first index (m) is omitted, then the slice starts at the beginning of the string.
- If the second index (n) is omitted, then the slice goes to the end of the string.
- If the first index is greater than or equal to the second index, the slice is an empty string.
- If both indices are omitted then the slice is a given string itself.
- Each character can be accessed by using indices within a square bracket.

Example 3.32:

```
str='Python Programming'
print("The Given String is",str)
print("The first character in the String is",str[0])
print("The String slice starting from 3rd to 5th position is",str[2:5])
print("The String slice starting from 3rd character is",str[2:])
print("The last character of the string(using negative index)is",str[-1])
print("The String slice from negative indices is",str[-5:])
print("The empty String is",str[3:3])
print("The Given String is",str[:])
print("Error:",str[18])
```

Output:

```
The Given String is Python Programming
The first character in the String is P
The String slice starting from 3rd to 5th position is tho
The String slice starting from 3rd character is thon Programming
The last character of the string(using negative index)is g
The String slice from negative indices is mming
The empty String is
The Given String is Python Programming
Traceback (most recent call last):
  File "C:\Python\Python37-32\s2.py", line 10, in <module>
    print("Error:",str[18])
IndexError: string index out of range
```

Example 3.33:

```
s="Python"
print(s[0])
print(s[2:5])
print(s[:4])
print(s[2:])
print(s[4:4])# empty string - blank line
print(s[4:3]) # empty string - blank line
print(s[:])
print(s[-3:])
print(s[:-3])
print(s[-6:-2])
```

Output:

```
P
tho
Pyth
thon

Python
hon
Pyt
Pyth
```

3.5.2 Immutability

- Strings are immutable i.e., characters can be accessed but it is not possible to change.
- If the string is created then it is not possible to modify.
- No assignments can be done but it is possible to update using concatenation operator.
- String can be deleted or removed using the keyword 'del'.
- operator cannot be used on the left side of an assignment.

Example 3.34: #NO ITEM ASSIGNMENT IN PYTHON

```
var="Python"
print(var)
var[2]="T"
```

Output:

```
Python
```

```
Traceback (most recent call last):
  File "C:/Python/Python37-32/s3.py", line 2, in <module>
    var[2]="T"
TypeError: 'str' object does not support item assignment
```

Example 3.35:

```
var="Python"
print(var)
del var[1]
```

Output:

```
Python
Traceback (most recent call last):
  File "C:/Python/Python37-32/s6.py", line 2, in <module>
    del var[1]
TypeError: 'str' object doesn't support item deletion
```

Example 3.36:

```
var="python"
del var
print(var)
```

Output:

```
Traceback (most recent call last):
  File "C:/Python/Python37-32/s3.py", line 3, in <module>
    print(var)
NameError: name 'var' is not defined
```

Example 3.37:

```
v1 = 'Python Programming'
print("Updated String:",'Welcome to '+ v1[0:])
```

Output:

```
Updated String: Welcome to Python Programming
```

3.5.3 String Operators

The following string operators are available in Python:

Table 3.2

Operator	**Description**	**Example a='Hello' and b='boys'**
+	Concatenation – joining two strings	a + b will give Helloboys
*	Repetition – Repeating the string given number of times.	a*2 will give HelloHello
[]	Slice – retrieve the character at given index	a[1] will give e
[:]	Range Slice – retrieve the characters with the specified range	a[1:4] will give ell
in	Membership - Returns *true* if a character exists in the given string	print('H' in a) will give *True*
not in	Membership - Returns *true* if a character does not exist in the given string	Print('M' not in a) will give *True*

Example 3.38:

```
a='I hate bitter food'
b="badly"
print("The Concatenation of the String is:",a+b)
print("The Repetition of the String is:",a*2)
print("The Slicing of the string is:",a[2])
print("The Slicing of the string is:",a[3:6])
print("The membership operator of the string is:",'t' in a)
print("The membership operator of the string is:",'B' not in b)
print("The membership operator of the string is:",'k' in a)
print("The membership operator of the string is:",'b' not in b)
```

Output:

```
The Concatenation of the String is: I hate bitter foodbadly
The Repetition of the String is: I hate bitter foodI hate bitter food
The Slicing of the string is: h
The Slicing of the string is: ate
The membership operator of the string is: True
The membership operator of the string is: True
The membership operator of the string is: False
The membership operator of the string is: False
```

3.5.4 String formatting Operator

Symbol used is %.

It is mainly used with print()

Table 3.3

Format Symbol	Conversion
%c	character
%s	string conversion via str() prior to formatting
%i	signed decimal integer
%d	signed decimal integer
%u	unsigned decimal integer
%o	octal integer
%x	hexadecimal integer (lowercase letters)
%X	hexadecimal integer (UPPERcase letters)
%e	exponential notation (with lowercase 'e')
%E	exponential notation (with UPPERcase 'E')
%f	floating point real number
%g	the shorter of %f and %e
%G	the shorter of %f and %E

For Example:

```
>>> name="John"
>>> age=42
>>> print("Name = %s, Age = %d"%(name,age))
Name = John, Age = 42
```

3.5.5 Escape sequences in string

"\" is a special character called the escape character. It is used to represent certain whitespace character.

Table 3.4

Escape Sequence	Description
\\	Backslash(\)
\'	Single quote(')
\"	Double quote(")
\b	ASCII Backspace
\f	ASCII Formfeed
\n	ASCII Linefeed(newline)
\r	ASCII Carriage Return
\t	ASCII Horizontal Tab(horizontal whitespace)

\v	ASCII Vertical Tab(vertical whitespace)
\ooo	Character with octal value ooo
\xHH	Character with hexadecimal value HH

3.5.6 String Methods and Functions

Many built-in string methods are available.

capitalize()	*center()*	*casefold()*	*count()*	*endswith()*	*encode()*
find()	*format()*	*index()*	*split()*	*rsplit()*	*title()*
zfill()	*isalpha()*	*isdecimal()*	*isdigit()*	*islower()*	*isupper()*
join()	*strip()*	*partition()*	*replace()*	*startswith()*	*isnumeric()*

1. *capitalize()*

- ***capitalize()*** method is used to capitalize the first letter in the string.
- This method does not take any argument.
- If first letter is already a capital letter or non-alphabet, then it returns the original string.

Syntax:

stringname.*capitalize*()

Example 3.39:

```
var1="python programming"
print("The result of capitalize function is",var1.capitalize())
```

Output:

```
The result of capitalize function is Python programming
```

2. *center()*

- ***center()*** method returns a string padded with the specified character with specified width.
- It does not modify the original string.

Syntax:

stringname.*center*(width,fillchar)

where width is length of the string & fillchar is a character to be filled.

Example 3.40:

```
str="Welcome"
print(str.center(18,'a'))
```

Output:

```
aaaaaWelcomeaaaaaa
```

3. *casefold()*

- ***casefold()*** method removes all case variations in a string. It is used to change all characters into lowercase.
- It is used for caseless matching.
- It does not take any parameters.

Syntax:

stringname.*casefold*()

Example 3.41:

```
a1="PYTHON programming"
print("The result of casefold function is",a1.casefold())
```

Output:

```
The result of casefold function is python programming
```

4. *count()*

count() method returns the number of occurrences of a substring in the range from starting index to ending index.

Syntax:

stringname.*count*(substring, [starting index], [ending index])

where substring is a string whose count is to be found, starting index (optional) is within the string where the search will start, ending index (optional) is within the string where the search will end. If the indexes are not specified the entire string is searched. The search is case-sensitive.

Example 3.42:

```
s="Engineering Knowledge"
print("The number of occurrences of the letter 'e' is",s.count('e'))
print("The number of occurrences of the letter 'e' from the index 6 to 18
            is",s.count('e',6,18))
```

Output:

```
The number of occurrences of the letter 'e' is 4
The number of occurrences of the letter 'e' from the index 6 to 18 is 2
```

5. *startswith()*

startswith() method returns *True* if a string starts with the specified prefix otherwise it returns *False*.

Syntax:

stringname.*startswith*(prefix, start, end)

where prefix is the string to be checked in the string; start and end are optional.

Example 3.43:

```
s="Computer Language"
```

```
res=s.startswith('Language',9)
print(res)
res=s.startswith('Language',2)
print(res)
```

Output:

```
True
False
```

6. *endswith()*

endswith() method returns *True* if a string ends with the specified suffix otherwise it returns *False*.

Syntax:

stringname.*endswith*(suffix,start,end)

where suffix is string to be checked in the string, start and end are optional.

Example 3.44:

```
s="English is just a language not knowledge"
result=s.endswith(" knowledge")
print(result)
result=s.endswith(" knowledge.")
print(result)
result=s.endswith("not")
print(result)
result=s.endswith("le",30,37)
print(result)
result=s.endswith("le",30,36)
print(result)
```

Output:

```
True
False
False
True
False
```

7. *find()*

find() method is used to return the lowest index of the substring (if found) otherwise it returns -1.

Syntax:

stringname.*find*(substring,start,end)

Example 3.45:

```
s="PYTHON programming"
print(s.find('PYTHON'))
print(s.find('Python'))
print(s.find('prog'))
```

Output:

```
0
-1
7
```

8. *index*()

***index*()** method is similar to *find*() but raises a value error exception if substring is not found.

Syntax:

stringname.*index*(substring,start,end)

Example 3.46:

```
s="welcome to python programming"
result=s.index('to python')
print("substring 'to python' at index",result)
```

Output:

```
substring 'to python' at index 8
```

9. *format*()

***format*()** method is used to make the presentation of output.

Syntax:

template.*format*(posarg1,posarg2,.....,keyarg0=v0,keyarg1=v1,....)

where posarg is positional argument and keyarg is keyword argument.

Template is a mixture of format codes with placeholders for the arguments. It takes two types of parameters:

1. Positional parameters

   Positional parameters is a list of parameters that can be accessed with the index of parameter inside the curly braces {index}

2. Keyword parameters

   Keyword parameters is a list of parameters of type key=value that can be accessed with the key of parameter inside the curly braces {key}

Example 3.47:

```
print("Hi {}! Welcome to {}".format("all","Python"))
#positional arguments
```

```
print("Hi {1}! Welcome to {0}".format("all","Python"))
#keyword arguments
print("Hi {key}! Welcome to {name}".format(key="all",name="Python"))
print("Hi {name}! Welcome to {key}".format(key="all",name="Python"))
#mixed arguments
print("Hi {0}! Welcome to {name}".format("all",name="Python"))
print("Hi {name}! Welcome to {0}".format("all",name="Python"))
#float arguments
print("The float number is {:f}".format(250.27))
#padding for float arguments
print("{:7.4f}".format(250.27))
#integer numbers with minimum width filled with zero
print("{:05d}".format(25))
```

Output:

```
Hi all! Welcome to Python
Hi Python! Welcome to all
Hi all! Welcome to Python
Hi Python! Welcome to all
Hi all! Welcome to Python
Hi Python! Welcome to all
The float number is 250.270000
250.2700
00025
```

10. *split()*

split() method breaks up a string at the specified separator and returns a list of strings.

Syntax:

stringname.*split*(separator,max)

where separator is the place where the split occurs & max is maximum number of splits.

Example 3.48:

```
new='abcdef'
print(new.split()) #separator is space
new='ab cd ef'
print(new.split()) #separator is space
items='black,blue,green'
print(items.split(',')) #separator is comma(,)
```

```
print(items.split(',',1)) #separator is comma(,) and maximum split is 1
print(items.split())#separator is space
new='a b c d e f'
print(new.split())#separator is whitespace
```

Output:

```
['abcdef']
['ab', 'cd', 'ef']
['black', 'blue', 'green']
['black', 'blue,green']
['black,blue,green']
['a', 'b', 'c', 'd', 'e', 'f']
```

11. *rsplit()*

rsplit() method is used to split a string from the right at the specified separator and return a list of strings.

Syntax:

stringname.*rsplit*(separator,max)

where separator is the place where the split occurs & max is maximum number of splits.

Example 3.49:

```
items='Beans,Peas,Carrot,Radish'
print(items.rsplit(',',2))
print(items.rsplit(',',1))
print(items.rsplit(',',5))
print(items.rsplit(',',0))
```

Output:

```
['Beans,Peas', 'Carrot', 'Radish']
['Beans,Peas,Carrot', 'Radish']
['Beans', 'Peas', 'Carrot', 'Radish']
['Beans,Peas,Carrot,Radish']
```

12. *title()*

***title*()** method is used to capitalize the first letter of each word in a given string. It does not take any parameter.

Syntax:

stringname.*title*()

Example 3.50:

```
s="python programming"
print(s.title())
```

Output:

```
Python Programming
```

13. *zfill()*

zfill() method is used to return a copy of the string with '0'(zero) characters padded to the left of the string in a total specified width.

Syntax:

stringname.*zfill*(width)

Example 3.51:

```
s="Hi! Python"
print(s.zfill(8)) #smaller width has no effect
print(s.zfill(11))
print(s.zfill(12))
print(s.zfill(15))
```

Output:

```
Hi! Python
0Hi! Python
00Hi! Python
00000Hi! Python
```

14. *isalnum()*

isalnum() method returns *True* if all the characters in the string are alphanumeric characters; otherwise it returns *False*. It does not take any parameters.

Syntax:

stringname.*isalnum*()

Example 3.52:

```
s="13June2020"
print(s.isalnum())
s="13 June 2020" #includes whitespace
print(s.isalnum())
s="June"
print(s.isalnum())
```

Output:

```
True
False
True
```

15. *isalpha()*

isalpha() method returns *True* if all the characters in the string are alphabet characters; otherwise it returns *False*. It does not take any parameters.

Syntax:

stringname.*isalpha*()

Example 3.53:

```
s="Python"
print(s.isalpha())
s="13June2020" #includes numeric characters
print(s.isalpha())
s="Python Programming" #includes whitespace character
print(s.isalpha())
```

Output:

```
True
False
False
```

16. *isdecimal()*

isdecimal() method returns *True* if all the characters in the string are digits from 0 to 9; otherwise it returns *False*. It does not take any parameters.

Syntax:

stringname.*isdecimal*()

Example 3.54:

```
s="144144"
print(s.isdecimal())
s="13June2020"
print(s.isdecimal())
s="144 144"
print(s.isdecimal())
```

Output:

```
True
False
False
```

17. *isdigit()*

isdigit() method returns *True* if all the characters in the string are digits from 0 to 9 or some unicode characters; otherwise it returns *False*. It does not take any parameters.

Syntax:

stringname.*isdigit*()

Example 3.55:

```
s="144144"
print(s.isdigit())
s="13June2020"
print(s.isdigit())
s="3"+"\u2082"# Unicode of subscript 2 is \u2082
print(s+" is digit")
print(s.isdigit())
s="144 144"
print(s.isdecimal())
```

Output:

```
True
False
3₂ is digit
True
False
```

18. *isnumeric*()

***isnumeric*()** method returns *True* if all the characters in the string are numeric characters; otherwise it returns *False*. It does not take any parameters. It accepts the Unicode character.

Syntax:

stringname.*isnumeric*()

A numeric character has the following properties:

- Numeric_Type=Decimal(0,1,2...)
- Numeric_Type=Digit(like subscript, superscript)
- Numeric_Type=Numeric(fraction, roman numerals, currency numerators)

Unicode of subscript 2 is \u2082, unicode of subscript 3 is \u2083, unicode of superscript 2 is \u00B2, unicode of superscript 3 is \u00B3, unicode of fraction ½ is \u00BD, ¾ is \u00BE, unicode of roman numerals I, II, III... is \u2160, \u2161, \u2162...

Example 3.56:

```
s="144144"
print(s.isnumeric())
s="\u00BD234"# ½234
```

```
print(s.isnumeric())
s="Python15"
print(s.isnumeric())
s="\u2165" # Roman numeral VI
print(s.isnumeric())
```

Output:

```
True
True
False
True
```

19. *islower()*

islower() method returns *True* if all the characters in the string are lowercase alphabets; otherwise it returns *False.*

Syntax:

stringname.*islower*()

Example 3.57:

```
s="python"
print(s.islower())
s="Python"
print(s.islower())
s="python  2nd  version"
print(s.islower())
```

Output:

```
True
False
True
```

20. *isupper()*

isupper() method returns *True* if all the characters in the string are uppercase alphabets; otherwise it returns *False.*

Syntax:

stringname.*isupper*()

Example 3.58:

```
s="PYTHON"
print(s.isupper())
s="Python"
print(s.isupper())
s="PYTHON  2ND  VERSION"
```

```
print(s.isupper())
if s.isupper()==True:
  print("All characters in s are uppercase")
else:
  print("s includes lowercase characters")
```

Output:

```
True
False
True
All characters in s are uppercase
```

21. *istitle()*

istitle() method returns *True* if the string is title case string; otherwise it returns *False*. It does not take any parameters.

Syntax:

string.*istitle*()

Example 3.59:

```
s="Python Programming"
print(s.istitle())
s="Python programming"
print(s.istitle())
s="PYTHON"
print(s.istitle())
```

Output:

```
True
False
False
```

22. *join()*

join() method is used to add the delimiter between every character in the string.

Syntax:

string1.*join*(string2)

where string1is the delimiter and string2 is the given string.

Example 3.60:

```
s1="->"
s2="123"
print(s1.join(s2))
```

Output:

```
1->2->3
```

23. *lower()*

lower() method is used to convert all uppercase characters in a string into lowercase characters. If there are no uppercase characters, it returns the original string.

Syntax:

string.*lower*()

Example 3.61:

```
s="PYTHON PROGRAMMING"
print(s.lower())
```

Output:

```
python programming
```

24. *upper()*

upper() method is used to convert all lowercase characters in a string into uppercase characters. If there are no lowercase characters, it returns the original string.

Syntax:

string.*upper*()

Example 3.62:

```
s="python programming"
print(s.upper())
```

Output:

```
PYTHON PROGRAMMING
```

25. *strip()*

strip() method is used to remove the unwanted whitespace from the string.

Syntax:

string.*strip*(chars)

chars(optional) is a string that is to be removed from the given string.

If the chars argument is not provided, all leading and trailing whitespaces are removed from the string.

lstrip() method is used to remove all leading whitespaces.

Syntax:

string.*lstrip*()

rstrip() method is used to remove all trailing whitespaces.

Syntax:

string.*rstrip*()

Example 3.63:

```
s="   Python Programming   "
print(s.strip())
s1="Python Programming"
print(s1.strip('Py'))
print(s1.strip('ng'))
print(s.lstrip())
print(s.rstrip())
```

Output:

```
Python Programming
thon Programming
Python Programmi
Python Programming
   Python Programming
```

26. *partition()*

partition() method is used to split the given string using the specified separator and return a tuple with three arguments.

Syntax:

string.*partition*(separator)

where separator is required otherwise it will throw TypeError.

Example 3.64:

```
s1="Learn-Python-Programming"
s2=s1.partition('-')
print(s2)
```

Output:

```
('Learn', '-', 'Python-Programming')
```

27. *replace()*

replace() method searches the specified string and replaces it with the new string. If the old substring is not found then it returns the original string.

Syntax:

string.*repalce*(old string,new string,count)

where count is the number of times to replace 'old string' with 'new string'

Example 3.65:

```
s1="Learn-Python-Programming"
s2=s1.replace('-',' ')
print(s2)
s2=s1.replace('-',' ',1)
print(s2)
```

Output:

```
Learn Python Programming
Learn Python-Programming
```

28. *max*()

***max*()** function returns the biggest alphabetical character from the string.

Syntax:

max(string)

Example 3.66:

```
s="programming"
print("Biggest Alphabet: ",max(s))
```

Output:

```
Biggest Alphabet:  r
```

29. *min*()

***min*()** function returns the smallest alphabetical character from the string.

Syntax:

min(string)

Example 3.67:

```
s="programming"
print("Smallest Alphabet: ",min(s))
```

Output:

```
Smallest Alphabet:  a
```

30. *len*()

***len*()** function returns the length of the given string.

Syntax:

len(string)

Example 3.68:

```
s="Python Programming"
print("Length of the string: ",len(s))
```

Output:

```
Length of the string:  18
```

3.5.7 String module

String module has numerous predefined functions to process the strings in Python. It contains some constants, utility functions and classes for string manipulations. This built-in module must be imported before using any of its functions, constants and classes. In recent versions, string module is not needed. All string operations are available as string methods which were discussed in the previous section.

Now, an example using string module is given below:

Example 3.69:

```
import string
s="Welcome to Python Programming"
print("Upper case:",str.upper(s))
print("Lower case:",str.lower(s))
print("Split:",str.split(s))
print("Join:"," ".join(s))
print("Replace:",str.replace(s,"Python","C"))
print("Find:",str.find(s,"Python"),str.find(s,"to"))
print("Count:",str.count(s,"o"))
```

Output:

```
Upper case: WELCOME TO PYTHON PROGRAMMING
Lower case: welcome to python programming
Split: ['Welcome', 'to', 'Python', 'Programming']
Join: W e l c o m e   t o   P y t h o n   P r o g r a m m i n g
Replace: Welcome to C Programming
Find: 11 8
Count: 4
```

3.5.8 Translation of character to other form:

maketrans() returns the translation table for passing to *translate*() that will map each character in 'fromch' into the character at the same position in 'toch'. Both 'fromch' and 'toch' must have the same length.

Syntax:

str.*maketrans*(fromch,toch)

Example 3.70:

```
import string
fromch="aeo"
toch="123"
newstr=str.maketrans(fromch,toch)
s="I love Python Programming"
print(s)
print(s.translate(newstr))
```

Output:

```
I love Python Programming
I l3v2 Pyth3n Pr3gr1mming
```

3.5.9 Constants:

Various string constants are available in string module.

Table 3.5

Constant	Value
string.ascii_letters	abcdefghijklmnopqrstuvwxyzABCDEFGHIJKLMNOPQRSTUV WXYZ
string.ascii_lowercase	Abcdefghijklmnopqrstuvwxyz
string.ascii_uppercase	ABCDEFGHIJKLMNOPQRSTUVWXYZ
string.digits	0123456789
string.octdigits	01234567
string.hexdigits	0123456789abcdefABCDEF
string.punctuation	!"#$%&'()*+,-./:;<=>?@[\]^_`{|}~

Example 3.71:

```
import string
print("String module constants")
print("Letters: ",string.ascii_letters)
print("Lowercase Letters: ",string.ascii_lowercase)
print("Uppercase Letters: ",string.ascii_uppercase)
print("Digits: ",string.digits)
print("OctDigits: ",string.octdigits)
print("Hex Digits: ",string.hexdigits)
print("Punctuation: ",string.punctuation)
```

Output:

```
String module constants
Letters:
abcdefghijklmnopqrstuvwxyzABCDEFGHIJKLMNOPQRSTUVWXYZ
Lowercase Letters:  abcdefghijklmnopqrstuvwxyz
Uppercase Letters:  ABCDEFGHIJKLMNOPQRSTUVWXYZ
Digits:  0123456789
OctDigits:  01234567
Hex Digits:  0123456789abcdefABCDEF
Punctuation:  !"#$%&'()*+,-./:;<=>?@[\]^_`{|}~
```

3.6 LISTS AS ARRAYS

1. Array:

Array is a data structure in which all the elements are of same data type. It can be imported using *import array* or *from array import ** (import all the functions in the array module). If *import array* is used then every time a function is called the array name must be specified like: array.function_name(). If *from array import ** is used then the function call need not be specified with array name; function_name(), will directly call the corresponding function.

Syntax:

arrayID=array(typecode,[initializers])

where arrayID is the name of an array, 'typecode' is the type of array, 'initializers' are the values which are to be stored into the arrayID as initial values.

Example 3.72:

```
from array import *
print("Integer Values: ")
a=array('i',[1,2,3,4]) # 'i' is a signed integer of size 2 bytes
for i in a:
    print(i)
print("Float Values: ")
a=array('f',[1,2,3,4]) # 'f' is a float
for i in a:
    print(i)
```

Output:

```
Integer Values:
1
2
3
4
Float Values:
1.0
2.0
3.0
4.0
```

2. Lists

A **list** is an ordered collection of elements which can be of **any data type**. Each element is separated using ','. It is mutable. The values in the list can be accessed using slice operator ([] and [:]) with indexes starting at '0' in the beginning of the list and negative indexes starting at '-1' from the end of the list.

del statement is used to delete an element.

List is similar to array where array is used to store the elements of same data type but list is used to store the elements of different data types.

Example 3.73:

```
a=[67,5.2,90,"yellow"]
for i in range(len(a)):
  print(a[i])
```

Output:

```
67
5.2
90
yellow
```

3.6.1 Accessing values in Lists:

Square brackets '[]' are used to access values in a list for slicing along with the index or indices to obtain the value available at that index.

For example, slice[m:n] - where m is the starting index which is included and n is the ending index which is excluded.

Example 3.74:

```
list1=[10,20,30,40,50]
print(list1[0])
print(list1[-1])
print(list1[2:4])
print(list1[:-2])
print(list1[-6])
```

Output:

```
10
50
[30, 40]
[10, 20, 30]
Traceback (most recent call last):
  File "C:/Python/Python37-32/a3.py", line 6, in <module>
    print(list1[-6])
IndexError: list index out of range
```

3.6.2 Updating list

Single or multiple elements can be updated in a list by giving the slice on the left-hand side of the assignment operator.

Elements can be added in a list with the *append()* method.

Example 3.75:

```
s=['Peas','Carrot','Beans','Radish','Brinjal']
print("Value at index 2:",s[2])
s[2]='Cabbage'
print(s)
s.append('Potato')
print(s)
```

Output:

```
Value at index 2: Beans
['Peas', 'Carrot', 'Cabbage', 'Radish', 'Brinjal']
['Peas', 'Carrot', 'Cabbage', 'Radish', 'Brinjal', 'Potato']
```

3.6.3 Deleting elements in a List

- *del* is used to delete an element at a particular index in the list.
- Element can be removed by stating its value using *remove*() method.

Example 3.76:

```
s=['Peas','Carrot','Beans','Radish','Brinjal']
print(s)
del s[2]
print(s)
s.remove('Radish')
print(s)
```

Output:

```
['Peas', 'Carrot', 'Beans', 'Radish', 'Brinjal']
['Peas', 'Carrot', 'Radish', 'Brinjal']
['Peas', 'Carrot', 'Brinjal']
```

3.7 ILLUSTRATIVE PROGRAMS

Prob. 3.7.1: Write a Python program to find the square root of a number using Newton's method.

Ans:

Let 'n' is any number, then the square root of n is found using the formula: root=0.5*(x+(n/x)) where 'x' is any guess that can be assumed 'n' or '1'. In the above formula 'x' is any assumed square root of 'n' and 'root' is the correct square root of 'n'

Program:

```
def newtonsqrt(n,x):
  while True:
    root=0.5*(x+(n/x))
    if root==x:
      break
    x=root
    print(x)
n=int(input("Enter an element to find the square root: "))
x=int(input("Enter the first estimate: "))
newtonsqrt(n,x)
```

Output:

```
Enter an element to find the square root: 16
Enter the first estimate: 3
4.166666666666666
4.003333333333334
4.000001387732445
4.000000000000241
4.0
```

Prob. 3.7.2: Write a Python program to find the GCD (Greatest Common Divisor) or HCF(Highest Common Factor) of two numbers.

Ans:

GCD of two numbers is the largest number that divides both of them. For example, GCD of 20 and 28 is 4.

Program:

```
def gcd(a,b):
  if(b==0):
    return a
  else:
    return gcd(b,a%b)
```

```
x=int(input("Enter the first number: "))
y=int(input("Enter the second number: "))
result=gcd(x,y)
print("GCD of %d and %d is: %d"%(x,y,result))
```

Output:

```
Enter the first number: 273
Enter the second number: 192
GCD of 273 and 192 is:  3
```

Prob. 3.7.3: Write a Python program to find the exponentiation of a number.

Ans:

Exponentiation (b^e) of a base number 'b' is the base number multiplied by itself the number of times indicated by the exponent 'e'.

Program:

```
def exp(b,e):
  if(e==1):
    return(b)
  if(e!=1):
    return(b*exp(b,e-1))
b=int(input("Enter the base: "))
e=int(input("Enter the exponential value: "))
print("Result:",exp(b,e))
```

Output:

```
Enter the base: 3
Enter the exponential value: 4
Result: 81
```

Prob. 3.7.4: Write a program to sum the array of numbers

Ans:

For example, let the given array a=[10,20,30,40,50]; then sum of the numbers in the given array is 10+20+30+40+50=150.

Program:

```
a=[] #'a' as a list
sum=0
n=int(input("Enter the number of elements: "))
for i in range(0,n):
  e=int(input("Enter the "+str(i)+"th element: "))
```

```
    a.append(e) #add the elements into the list
for i in a:
    sum=sum+i
print("Sum of the array of numbers in the list is :",sum)
```

Output:

```
Enter the number of elements: 5
Enter the 0th element: 10
Enter the 1th element: 20
Enter the 2th element: 30
Enter the 3th element: 40
Enter the 4th element: 50
Sum of the array of numbers in the list is : 150
```

Prob. 3.7.5: Write a Python program to find an element in a list using linear search/sequential search.

Ans:

A linear search or sequential search is a method for finding an element within a list. This method checks the elements one by one in the list until a match is found. If a match is not found, it means the required element is not in the list.

Program:

```
def linearsearch(list,s):
    length=len(list)
    for i in range(0,length):
        if list[i]==s:
            return(i+1)
            break
        else:
        return(-1)
a=[]#'a' as a list
sum=0
n=int(input("Enter the number of elements: "))
for i in range(0,n):
    e=int(input("Enter the "+str(i)+"th element: "))
    a.append(e)#add the elments into the list
search=int(input("Enter the number to be searched: "))
res=linearsearch(a,search)
if res==-1:
```

```
        print(search," is not found in the list")
    else:
        print(search," is found in the list at the position ",res)
```

Output:

Case 1:

```
Enter the number of elements: 5
Enter the 0th element: 34
Enter the 1th element: 78
Enter the 2th element: 12
Enter the 3th element: 65
Enter the 4th element: 43
Enter the number to be searched: 65
65  is found in the list at the position  4
```

Case 2:

```
Enter the number of elements: 5
Enter the 0th element: 34
Enter the 1th element: 78
Enter the 2th element: 12
Enter the 3th element: 65
Enter the 4th element: 43
Enter the number to be searched: 99
99  is not found in the list
```

Prob. 3.7.6: Write a Python program to find an element in a list using Binary search.

Ans:

Binary search is a search method used to find the given element within a sorted array. The method first finds the middle position of the array. Then compares the given element with the middle element of the array. If a match is found, its position is returned. Otherwise, it is checked if the given element is less than or greater than the middle element. If it is less, then the search continues on the left side of the array; otherwise search continues on right side of the array using the same procedure.

Program:

```
def binarysearch(list,s):
    first = 0
    last = len(list)-1
    found=False
    while(first<=last and not found):
```

```
        mid = (first+last)//2
        #mid=int(mid) #gives mid a rounded value if it is in float
        if (s==list[mid]):
          return mid
        elif(s<list[mid]):
          last=mid-1
        else:
          first=mid+1
  return found
a=[]#'a' as a list
sum=0
n=int(input("Enter the number of elements: "))
for i in range(0,n):
  e=int(input("Enter the "+str(i)+"th element: "))
  a.append(e)#add the elments into the list
a.sort() # 'a' is a sorted list
print("Sorted List:")
print(a)
search=int(input("Enter the number to be searched: "))
position = binarysearch(a,search)
if(position!=0):
  print("Entered number %d is present at position:
  %d"%(search,position+1))
else:
  print("Entered number %d is not present in the list"%search)
```

Output:

Case 1:

```
Enter the number of elements: 5
Enter the 0th element: 34
Enter the 1th element: 78
Enter the 2th element: 12
Enter the 3th element: 65
Enter the 4th element: 43

Sorted List:
[12, 34, 43, 65, 78]
Enter the number to be searched: 78
Entered number 78 is present at position: 5
```

Case 2:

```
Enter the number of elements: 5
Enter the 0th element: 34
Enter the 1th element: 78
Enter the 2th element: 12
Enter the 3th element: 65
Enter the 4th element: 43
Sorted List:
[12, 34, 43, 65, 78]
Enter the number to be searched: 10
Entered number 10 is not present in the list
```

Prob. 3.7.7: Write a Python program to find the square root, gcd and exponentiation using built-in funcions.

Ans:

Program:

```
import math
print("Square Root")
num=int(input("Enter the number: "))
result=math.sqrt(num)
print("Square root of %d is: %d"%(num,result))
print("Greatest Common Divisor")
x=int(input("Enter the first number: "))
y=int(input("Enter the second number: "))
result=math.gcd(x,y)
print("GCD of %d and %d is: %d"%(x,y,result))
print("Exponentiation")
b=int(input("Enter the base: "))
e=int(input("Enter the exponential value: "))
result=math.pow(b,e)
print("Exponentiation of %d power %d is: %d"%(b,e,result))
```

Output:

```
Square Root
Enter the number: 100
Square root of 100 is: 10
Greatest Common Divisor
Enter the first number: 273
```

```
Enter the second number: 192
GCD of 273 and 192 is: 3
Exponentiation
Enter the base: 3
Enter the exponential value: 4
Exponentiation of 3 power 4 is: 81
```

Short Questions

1. Define Boolean expression with example.

A **boolean expression** is an expression whose value is either *True* or *False*. The values *True* and *False* are called Boolean values.

Example :

```
>>> 5 == 6
False
```

True and *False* are special values that belong to the type *bool*; they are not strings.

2. What are the different types of operators?

- Arithmetic Operators (+, -, *, /, %, **, //)
- Relational operators (== , !=, < >, < , > , <=, >=)
- Assignment Operators (=, += , *= , - =, /=, %= ,**=)
- Logical Operators (*and, or, not*)
- Membership Operators (*in, not in*)
- Bitwise Operator (& (and), | (or) , ^ (binary Xor), ~(binary 1's complement , << (binary left shift), >> (binary right shift))
- Identity(*is, is not*)

3. Explain the modulus operator with example.

The **modulus operator** works on integers and yields the remainder when the first operand is divided by the second. In Python, the modulus operator is a percentage sign (%).

Example:

```
>>> remainder = 7 % 3
>>>print(remainder)
 1
>>> remainder = 2 % 5
>>>print(remainder)
2
```

4. Explain the relational operators.

Relational Operators are used to compare two values and return *True* or *False*. It is useful for decision making. It is also called as comparison operator.

Relational Operators in Python:

Operator	Meaning	Example	Explanation
>	Greater than	a>b	True if a is greater than b
<	Less than	a<b	True if a is less than b
>=	Greater than or equal to	a>=b	True if a is greater than or equal to b
<=	Less than or equal to	a<=b	True if a is less than or equal to b
==	Equal to	a==b	True if a is equal to b
!=	Not equal to	a!=b	True if a is not equal to b

Example: ***example2.py***

```
a=int(input('Enter the value of a: '))
b=int(input('Enter the value of b: '))
print('a>b is ', a>b) # true if a>b
print('a<b is ', a<b) # true if a<b
print('a>=b is ', a>=b) # true if a>=b
print('a<=b is ', a<=b) # true if a<=b
print('a==b is ', a==b) # true if a==b
print('a!=b is ', a!=b) # true if a!=b
```

Output:

```
Enter the value of a: 12
Enter the value of b: 12
a>b is False
a<b is False
a>=b is True
a<=b is True
a==b is True
a!=b is False
```

5. Explain Logical operators.

Logical operators are used on one or more relational or Boolean expressions. There are three logical operators: *and*, *or*, and *not*. For example, $x > 0$ *and* $x < 10$ is *True* only if x is greater than 0 and less than 10. n%2 == 0 *or* n%3 == 0 is *True* if either of the conditions is *True*, that is, if the number is divisible by 2 or 3. Finally, the *not* operator negates a Boolean expression, so *not*(x > y) is *True* if x > y is *False*, that is, if x is less than or equal to y. Non-zero number is said to be *True* in Boolean expressions.

6. What is conditional execution?

The ability to check a condition and change the behavior of the program accordingly is called conditional execution.

Example:

***if* statement:**

The simplest form of if statement is:

Syntax:

```
if condition:
    statement
```

Example:

```
if x > 0:
    print( 'x is positive')
```

The boolean expression after 'if' is called the condition. If it is *True*, then the indented statement gets executed. If not, nothing happens.

7. What is an alternative execution?

In the *if* statement, if the condition is true then it will execute the true block statements otherwise it will execute false block statements. This is an alternative execution.

Syntax:

```
if condition:
        true block statements
else:
        false block statements
```

Example:

```
if x%2 == 0:
        print( 'x is even')
else:
        print( 'x is odd')
```

8. What are chained conditionals?

Chained conditional is used to test more than one condition.

elif is short form for else-if. It is a multipath decision statement. It is used to check multiple conditions. The conditions are executed from the top to the bottom. If the condition 1 is false it checks the condition 2 of the next *elif* block and so on.

If all the conditions are false then the else statement is executed. *if-elif* contains one *else* block. But it can have multiple *elif* blocks.

Syntax:

```
if condition 1:
        statements
elif condition 2:
        statements
.
.
.
elif condition n:
        statements
else:
        statements
```

Example:

```
if x < y:
   print ('x is less  than y')
elif x > y:
        print( 'x is greater than y')
else:
        print( 'x and y are equal')
```

9. Explain while loop with example.

while is an entry-controlled loop. It executes a block of statements repeatedly until the condition becomes *False*.

Syntax:

```
while condition:
        block of statements
next statement
```

The flow of execution for a *while* statement:

1. Evaluate the condition, yielding *True* or *False*.
2. If the condition is false, exit the while statement and continue execution at the next statement.
3. If the condition is true, execute the body and then go back to step 1

Example:

```
count=0
while count<5:
```

```
print("The count value is",count)
count=count+1
```

10. Explain 'for loop' with example.

***for* loop** is used to execute a sequence of statements multiple times. If the number of times 'n' that a set statements is to be executed is already known then *for* loop is chosen.

Syntax:

```
for val in sequence:
        statements
```

- 'val' is a variable that takes value of the item inside the sequence on each iteration.
- Loop continues until the last item in the sequence is reached.
- *for* loop contains initialization and condition part, but increment and decrement need not be defined in Python.

Example:

```
x = 4
for i in range(0, x):
  print i
```

11. What is a break statement?

break statement is used to bring the control out of the loop. It terminates the loop statement and transfers execution to the statement immediately following the loop.

Syntax:

break

Example:

```
for x in range(1,10):
  if x==5:
    break
  print("x=",x)
```

12. What is a continue statement?

Continue statement is used to return the control to the beginning of the loop. It skips all remaining statements in the current iteration of the loop and moves the control back to the top of the loop. It can be used both in while and for loops.

Syntax:

continue

Example:

```
for x in range(1,10):
```

```
if x==5:
   continue
print("x=",x)
```

13. Compare return value and composition.

Return Value	Composition
1. *Return* statement gives back a value or control returns to the caller of the function. 2. It causes the function to exit and it may return a value to its caller.	1. The ability of calling one function from within another function is called as composition. 2. It is a way of combining functions such that the result of the called function is passed as the argument of the calling function.

14. What is recursion?

Recursion is a process of calling a function by itself again and again until some condition is satisfied. A function called by itself is called as a recursive function.

Example: #Finding factorial of a given number n

```
def factorial(n):
   if n==1:
      return 1
   else:
      return n*factorial(n-1)
print(factorial(5))
```

15. Explain global and local scope.

The scope of a variable refers to the places that we can see or access a variable. If we define a variable on the top of the script or module, the variable is called global variable. The variables that are defined inside a class or function is called local variable.

Example: #local scope

```
def my_local():
      a=10
      print("This is local variable")
```

Example: # global scope

```
a=10
def my_global():
          print("a is global variable a=",a)
```

16. Compare string and string slices

String	String Slices
1. String is a sequence of characters enclosed within single quotes (' '), double quotes (" "), triple single quotes (''' ''') or triple double quotes(""" """).	1. A part of a string is called as slice. Slice is used to take sub parts of either a list or a string. [] is used as a slice operator.

2. For Example,
>>> fruit = ' banana '
>>> print(fruit)
Banana
	2. For Example ,
	>>> s ='Monty Python'
	>>> print s[0:5]
	Monty
	>>> print s[6:12]
	Python

17. Define string immutability

- Strings are immutable i.e., characters can be accessed but it is not possible to change.
- If the string is created then it is not possible to modify.
- No assignments can be done but it is possible to update.
- String can be deleted or removed using the keyword 'del'.
- [] operator cannot be used on the left side of an assignment.

Example:

```
var="Python"
print(var)
var[2]="T" # TypeError: 'str' object does not support item
assignment
```

18. Mention a few string functions

max() function returns the biggest alphabetical character from the string.

Syntax:

max(string)

min() function returns the smallest alphabetical character from the string.

Syntax:

min(string)

len() function returns the length of the given string.

Syntax:

len(string)

19. What are string methods?

String methods take arguments and return a value. To use a method it is annexed to the string with a dot.

For Example,

```
s="python programming"
print(s.upper())
```

Output:

```
PYTHON PROGRAMMING
```

20. Explain string module.

String module is a collection of numerous predefined functions to process strings in python. It contains some constants, utility functions and classes for string manipulations. This built-in module must be imported before using any of its functions, constants and classes.

Example:

```
import string
s="Welcome to Python Programming"
print("Upper case:",str.upper(s))
print("Lower case:",str.lower(s))
print("Split:",str.split(s))
```

21. What is the purpose of pass statement?

A ***pass*** statement is an explicit way of telling the interpreter to do nothing.

Example:

```
def bar():
        pass
```

If the function bar() is called, it does absolutely nothing.

Unsolved Exercises

1. If you are given three sticks, you may or may not be able to arrange them in a triangle. For example, if one of the sticks is 12 inches long and the other two are one inch long, it is clear that you will not be able to get the short sticks to meet in the middle. For any three lengths, there is a simple test to see if it is possible to form a triangle:

   If any of the three lengths is greater than the sum of the other two, then you cannot form a triangle. Otherwise, you can.

   (i) Write a function named is_triangle that takes three integers as arguments, and that prints either "Yes" or "No" depending on whether you can or cannot form a triangle from sticks with the given lengths.

(ii) Write a function that prompts the user to input three stick lengths, converts them to integers, and uses is_triangle to check whether sticks with the given lengths can form a triangle.

2. A number, a, is a power of b if it is divisible by b and a/b is a power of b. Write a function called is_power that takes parameters a and b and returns *True* if a is a power of b.
3. Write a Python program to find out the roots of a quadratic equation.
4. Write a Python program to print multiplication table for a given number n.
5. Write a Python program to compute sum of first n natural numbers.
6. Write a Python program to determine whether a number is palindrome or not.
7. Write a Python program to print all the possible combinations of 2, 3, and 4
8. Write a Python program to reverse the digits of a number.
9. Write a Python program to determine whether a given number is prime or not.
10. Write a Python program to print numbers upto N which are not divisible by 3, 6, and 9, eg., 1, 2, 4, 5, 7, ...

UNIT IV
COMPOUND DATA: LISTS, TUPLES, DICTIONARIES

Contents

Lists, list operations, list slices, list methods, list loop, mutability, aliasing, cloning lists, list parameters; Tuples, tuple assignment, tuple as return value; Dictionaries: operations and methods; advanced list processing - list comprehension, Illustrative programs: selection sort, insertion sort, merge sort, histogram.

4.1 LIST

A list is a sequence of values. These values are separated by commas and enclosed within square brackets ([ ]). The values can be of any type such as strings, tuples, lists, dictionaries, functions, file objects, and any type of number. A list can be indexed from its front (0, 1, 2, ...) or from back(-1, -2, - 3, ...). Lists are mutable.

Sub segment or *slice* of the list is referred by using slice notation [:]. It displays the values from starting index to previous of end index.

Each and every item has its unique index. The items can be of mixed type.

Example 4.1:

```
List1= [1, 2, 3]
List2 = [ ] #empty list
List3= [ [4,8],List1]
print (List1)
print (List2)
print (List3)
```

Output:

```
[1, 2, 3]
[]
[[4, 8], [1, 2, 3]]
```

4.1.1 List indexing

List elements are indexed from left to right starting at 0 and it is called as positive indexing. List elements are indexed also from right to left starting at -1 and it is called as negative indexing.

Two type of indexing:

1. Positive indexing / Forward indexing
   Positive indices start from the beginning of the list and move towards right.
2. Negative indexing / Backward indexing
   Negative indices start from the end of the list and move towards left.

Forward	**0**	**1**	**2**	**3**	**4**	**5**	
	P	Y	T	H	O	N	
	-6	**-5**	**-4**	**-3**	**-2**	**-1**	**Backward**

Example 4.2:

```
list1= [1, 2, 3, 4, 5]
print("List: ",list1)
print("list1[2]  = ",list1[2])
print("list1[-2] = ",list1[-2])
print("list1[0]  = ",list1[0])
print("list1[-1] = ",list1[-1])
```

Output:

```
List:  [1, 2, 3, 4, 5]
list1[2]  =  3
list1[-2] =  4
list1[0]  =  1
list1[-1] =  5
```

4.1.2 List Operations

List can perform the operations like a string such as concatenation, indexing, slicing, the *len* function etc.

1. Concatenation Operator (+):

The concatenation operator (+) is used to add a list of elements to another list.

Example 4.3:

```
l1=[10,20,30,40]+[50,60,70]
l2=l1+["Numbers"]
print("[10,20,30,40] + [50,60,70] = ",l1)
print("[10,20,30,40,50,60,70] + [\"Numbers\"] = ",l2)
```

Output:

```
[10,20,30,40] + [50,60,70] =  [10, 20, 30, 40, 50, 60, 70]
[10,20,30,40,50,60,70] + ["Numbers"] =  [10, 20, 30, 40, 50, 60, 70, 'Numbers']
```

2. Repetition Operator (*):

'*' operator is used for repetition. It creates a new list by repeating the existing list the given number of times.

Example 4.4:

```
list1=[1,2,3,4]*2
list2=["&"]*3
print(list1)
print(list2)
```

Output:

```
[1, 2, 3, 4, 1, 2, 3, 4]
['&', '&', '&']
```

3. len():

len(s) returns the number of elements in a sequence s.

Example 4.5:

```
list1=[1,2,3,4]
print(len(list1))
```

Output:

```
4
```

4. max() & min():

max(s) returns the largest value in a sequence 's' and min(s) returns the smallest value in a sequence 's'

Example 4.6:

```
list1=[10,20,30,40]
print("Maximum value in list1: ",max(list1))
print("Minimum value in list1: ",min(list1))
```

Output:

```
Maximum value in list1:  40
Minimum value in list1:  10
```

5. Membership Operator (*in*):

The *in* operator is used to test the membership. It returns *True* if the element is present in a list otherwise it returns *False*.

Example 4.7:

```
list1=[1,2,3,4]
print("List1: ",list1)
```

```
print("2 in list1: ",2 in list1)
print("6 in list1: ",6 in list1)
```

Output:

```
List1:  [1, 2, 3, 4]
2 in list1:  True
6 in list1:  False
```

6. Inverse Operator (*not in*) or Membership Operator:

The inverse operator *not in* returns *False* if the element is present in a list otherwise it returns *True.*

Example 4.8:

```
list1=[1,2,3,4]
print("List1: ",list1)
print("2 not in list1: ",2 not in list1)
print("6 not in list1: ",6 not in list1)
```

Output:

```
List1:  [1, 2, 3, 4]
2 not in list1:  False
6 not in list1:  True
```

7. list():

list() function is used to convert a sequence (tuple or string) into list.

Example 4.9:

```
s="Python"
t=(1,2,3,4)
print("String s: ",s)
print("Convert string into list: ",list(s))
print("Tuple t: ",t)
print("Convert tuple into list : ",list(t))
```

Output:

```
String s:  Python
Convert string into list:  ['P', 'y', 't', 'h', 'o', 'n']
Tuple t:  (1, 2, 3, 4)
Convert tuple into list :  [1, 2, 3, 4]
```

4.1.3 List Slices

A subset of elements present in a list is called as list slice. The operator [m:n] returns the part of the list from m^{th} index to n^{th} index, including the element at m^{th} index but excluding the element at n^{th} index.

If the 1st index is omitted then the slice starts at the beginning of the list.

If the 2nd index is omitted then the slice goes to the end of the list.

If both indices are omitted then the slice is the given list itself.

Example 4.10:

```
x = ["one", "two", "three", "four"]
print("List x is: ",x)
print("x[0]   : ",x[0])
print("x[2]   : ",x[2])
print("x[-1]  : ",x[-1])
print("x[-2]  : ",x[-2])
print("x[1:-1] : ",x[1:-1])
print("x[0:3]  : ",x[0:3])
print("x[-2:-1]: ",x[-2:-1])
print("x[:3]   : ",x[:3])
print("x[2:]   : ",x[2:])
print("x[:]    : ",x[:])
```

Output:

```
List x is:  ['one', 'two', 'three', 'four']
x[0]    : one
x[2]    : three
x[-1]   : four
x[-2]   : three
x[1:-1] : ['two', 'three']
x[0:3]  : ['one', 'two', 'three']
x[-2:-1]: ['three']
x[:3]   : ['one', 'two', 'three']
x[2:]   : ['three', 'four']
x[:]    : ['one', 'two', 'three', 'four']
```

1. Change the elements in a list:

Lists are mutable. List elements can be changed unlike string or tuple. Assignment operator(=) is used to change an item or range of items.

Example 4.11:

```
list1=[0, 2, 3, 4, 5, 6, 7, 8]
print(list1)
list1[0]=1 # element 0 is changed to 1
```

```
print(list1)
list1[3:5]=[] #elements 4,5 are made empty
print(list1)
```

Output:

```
[0, 2, 3, 4, 5, 6, 7, 8]
[1, 2, 3, 4, 5, 6, 7, 8]
[1, 2, 3, 6, 7, 8]
```

2. Delete or remove elements from a list

del keyword is used to delete an element, more than one element or an entire list.

Example 4.12:

```
list1=[1, 2, 3, 4, 5, 6, 7, 8]
print(list1)
del list1[2]#delete an element at index 2
print(list1)
del list1[3:5]#delete the elements at indices 3 and 4
print(list1)
del list1#delete the entire list
print(list1)#list not defined
```

Output:

```
[1, 2, 3, 4, 5, 6, 7, 8]
[1, 2, 4, 5, 6, 7, 8]
[1, 2, 4, 7, 8]
Traceback (most recent call last):
  File "C:/Python/Python37-32/l12.py", line 8, in <module>
    print(list1)
NameError: name 'list1' is not defined
```

4.1.4. List Methods

Methods in lists are used to manipulate the data quickly. Python provides the following methods that work on lists:

1. ***append()***

append() method is used to add an element to the end of the list. It does not return any value.

Syntax:

```
Listname.append(element)
```

Example 4.13:

```
list1=["Joash",'Pudukkottai',18]
print("Before Append: ",list1)
list1.append('CSE')
print("After Append: ",list1)
```

Output:

```
Before Append: ['Joash', 'Pudukkottai', 18]
After Append: ['Joash', 'Pudukkottai', 18, 'CSE']
```

2. ***extend()***

extend() method is used to add all elements of a list to another list. It does not return any value. It is similar to concatenation.

Syntax:

```
Firstlist.extend(secondlist)
```

Example 4.14:

```
list1=[10,20,30]
print("Before Extend: ",list1)
list2=[40,50,60]
list1.extend(list2)
print("After Extend: ",list1)
```

Output:

```
Before Extend: [10, 20, 30]
After Extend: [10, 20, 30, 40, 50, 60]
```

3. ***insert()***

insert() method is used to insert the given element at the given index in a list. It does not return any value.

Syntax:

```
Listname.insert(index,element)
```

Example 4.15:

```
list1=[10,20,30]
print("Before Insert: ",list1)
list1.insert(2,25)
print("After Insert: ",list1)
```

Output:

```
Before Insert: [10, 20, 30]
After Insert: [10, 20, 25, 30]
```

4. ***remove()***

remove() method is used to remove an element from the list. It does not return any value.

Syntax:

```
Listname.remove(element)
```

Example 4.16:

```
list1=[18,'Ram','CSE','Pudukkottai']
print("Before Remove: ",list1)
list1.remove('CSE')
print("After Remove: ",list1)
```

Output:

```
Before Remove:  [18, 'Ram', 'CSE', 'Pudukkottai']
After Remove:  [18, 'Ram', 'Pudukkottai']
```

5. ***pop()***

pop() method is used to remove an element. If this method does not contain any argument then it removes the element at the end of the list otherwise it removes the element at the specified index.

Syntax:

```
Listname.pop(index)
```

where index is optional.

Example 4.17:

```
list1=[18,'Ram','CSE','Pudukkottai']
print("Before Pop: ",list1)
list1.pop() #Removes the last element
print("After Pop without index: ",list1)
list1.pop(1) #Removes the element at the specified index
print("After Pop with index 1: ",list1)
```

Output:

```
Before Pop:  [18, 'Ram', 'CSE', 'Pudukkottai']
After Pop without index:  [18, 'Ram', 'CSE']
After Pop with index 1:  [18, 'CSE']
```

6. ***del()***

del() method is used to delete an element with specified index or delete an entire list.

Syntax:

del(Listname[index])

or

del(Listname[a:b]) # This method deletes all the elements in range starting from index 'a' to 'b-1'.

Example 4.18:

```
list1=[10,20,30,40,50,60,70]
print("Before del: ",list1)
del(list1[3]) #element at index 3 is deleted
print("After del: ",list1)
del(list1[1:3])#elements at indices 1,2 are deleted
print("After del: ",list1)
del list1 #list1is deleted
print(list1)
```

Output:

```
Before del:  [10, 20, 30, 40, 50, 60, 70]
After del:  [10, 20, 30, 50, 60, 70]
After del:  [10, 50, 60, 70]
Traceback (most recent call last):
  File "C:/Python/Python37-32/l19.py", line 8, in <module>
    print(list1)
NameError: name 'list1' is not defined
```

7. ***sort()***

sort() method is used to arrange the elements in a list in ascending or descending order. This method overwrites the previous data. So, if the original list is needed a copy of the list should be preserved under a different name. This method does not return a value.

Syntax:

Listname.sort(reverse=True|false, key=myFun)

Where, reverse is optional. *reverse = True* will sort the list in descending order. Default is *reverse=False*. key is optional. A function myFun is used to specify the sorting criteria.

Example 4.19:

```
def myFun(e):
  return(len(e))
list1=[50,75,10,25,65,30]
print("Before sort: ",list1)
list1.sort()
print("After sort: ",list1)
```

```
list2=['defg','abc','xy','mnopqr','hijkl']
print("Before sort: ",list2)
list2.sort(key=myFun)
print("After sort using key argument: ",list2)
```

Output:

```
Before sort:  [50, 75, 10, 25, 65, 30]
After sort:  [10, 25, 30, 50, 65, 75]
Before sort:  ['defg', 'abc', 'xy', 'mnopqr', 'hijkl']
After sort using key argument:  ['xy', 'abc', 'defg', 'hijkl', 'mnopqr']
```

8. *reverse()*

reverse() method is used to reverse the entire list.

Syntax:

```
Listname.reverse()
```

Example 4.20:

```
list1=[50,75,10,'xy',65,'ab']
print("Before reverse: ",list1)
list1.reverse()
print("After reverse: ",list1)
```

Output:

```
Before reverse:  [50, 75, 10, 'xy', 65, 'ab']
After reverse:  ['ab', 65, 'xy', 10, 75, 50]
```

9. *count()*

count() method returns the number of occurrences of an element in a specified list.

Syntax:

```
Listname.count(element)
```

Example 4.21:

```
list1=[50,75,10,50,65,'ab','xy','ab',50]
print("List1: ",list1)
print("Number of occurrences of 50 in list1:",list1.count(50))
print("Number of occurrences of 'ab' in list1:",list1.count('ab'))
```

Output:

```
List1:  [50, 75, 10, 50, 65, 'ab', 'xy', 'ab', 50]
Number of occurrences of 50 in list1: 3
Number of occurrences of 'ab' in list1: 2
```

10. *index()*

index() method returns the index of the element present in the list.

Syntax:

Listname.index(element,start index,end index)

where start index and end index are optional; when included they specify the range of search.

Example 4.22:

```
list1=[50,75,'ab',25,'xy',80,20,'ab']
print("List1: ",list1)
print("Element 'ab' at index:",list1.index('ab'))
print("Element 'ab' from the index 3 to 7(8-1):",list1.index('ab',3,8))
```

Output:

```
List1:  [50, 75, 'ab', 25, 'xy', 80, 20, 'ab']
Element 'ab' at index: 2
Element 'ab' from the index 3 to 7(8-1): 7
```

11. *copy()*

copy() method returns a shallow copy of the list. (A reference of object is copied in new object. It means that any changes made to a copy of object do reflect in the original object.)

Syntax:

Newlistname=Listname.copy()

Example 4.23:

```
list1=[50,75,21.5,45,38]
c=list1.copy()
print("List c is the copy of list1: ",c)
```

Output:

```
List c is the copy of list1:  [50, 75, 21.5, 45, 38]
```

4.1.5 List Loops

An element in the list can be accessed by traversing the list using *for* loop. The following snippet shows the use of *for* loop to access the elements in a list.

Example 4.24:

```
list1=[50,75,21.5,45,38]
for i in list1:
  print(i)
```

Output:

```
50
75
21.5
```

```
45
38
```

Example 4.25: The following code displays the output in format:

```
list1=[50,75,21.5,45,38]
j=0
for i in list1:
  print("Element at index {0} is {1}".format(j,i))
  j=j+1
```

Output:

```
Element at index 0 is 50
Element at index 1 is 75
Element at index 2 is 21.5
Element at index 3 is 45
Element at index 4 is 38
```

range() and *len()* functions are also used to access the elements in a list.

Example 4.26:

```
list1=[50,75,21.5,45,38]
for i in range(len(list1)):
  print(list1[i])
```

Output:

```
50
75
21.5
45
38
```

Here, *len*() function is used to return the number of elements in the list and *range*() function returns the list of indices from 0 to n-1, where 'n' is the length of the list.

4.1.6 Mutability

List is mutable. It is possible to change the elements without recreating it. Elements can be replaced by using a slice operator on the left hand side of the assignment operator (=) to change an element or a range of elements. Elements can be added by using the methods such as *insert, append* or *extend*. Elements can be deleted by using the methods such as *del* or *remove*.

Example 4.27:

```
list1=[1,2,3,4,5]
```

```
print("Original list:",list1)
for i in range(len(list1)):
  list1[i]=list1[i]*2
print("All elements are changed",list1)
list1[1:4]=6,9,12
print("Elements are changed from index 1 to 3:",list1)
```

Output:

```
Original list: [1, 2, 3, 4, 5]
All elements are changed [2, 4, 6, 8, 10]
Elements are changed from index 1 to 3: [2, 6, 9, 12, 10]
```

4.1.7 Aliasing

When a list is created it becomes an object. When two lists are created two different objects are created even if all the elements are identical. For example,

```
list1=[1,2]
list2=[1,2]
print(list1 is list2)
```

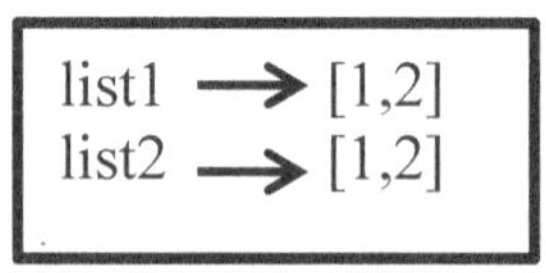

Output:

```
False
```

Here, two lists ***list1*** and ***list2*** are equivalent because they have same elements. But they are not identical since they are not the same object.

If two objects are identical then they are equivalent. If two objects are equivalent then they are not necessarily identical.

When two identifiers are made to refer to the same variable or value, then it is called as aliasing.

For example,

```
list1=[1,2]
list2= list1
print(list1 is list2)
```

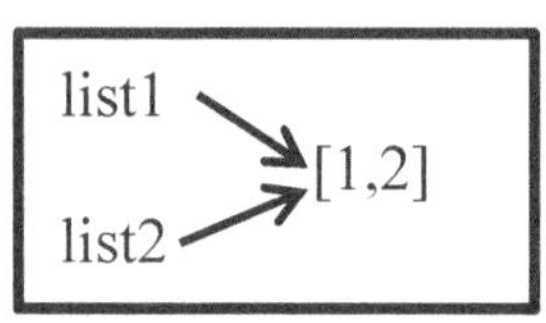

Output:

```
True
```

Modifications done in one object affect the other object also.

For example,

```
list1=[1,2]
list2=list1
print("List1 is:",list1)
print("List2 is:",list2)
```

```
list1[0]=10
print("List1 is:",list1)
print("List2 is:",list2)
list2[1]=20
print("List1 is:",list1)
print("List2 is:",list2)
```

Output:

```
List1 is: [1, 2]
List2 is: [1, 2]
List1 is: [10, 2]
List2 is: [10, 2]
List1 is: [10, 20]
List2 is: [10, 20]
```

When it is required to prevent aliasing, a new object is created and the contents of the original are copied to the new object.

For example,

```
list1=[1,2]
list2=[]
for i in list1:
  list2.append(i)
print("List1 is:",list1)
print("List2 is:",list2)
list1[0]=10
print("After Modification:")
print("List1 is:",list1)
print("List2 is:",list2)
```

Output:

```
List1 is: [1, 2]
List2 is: [1, 2]
After Modification:
List1 is: [10, 2]
List2 is: [1, 2]
```

4.1.8 Cloning Lists

Cloning means creating a replica of the original list. It is a process of making a copy of the list without modifying the original list.

When changes are done in the cloning list they will not affect the original list. There are various methods used for cloning a list.

1. Clone by assignment
2. Clone by slicing
3. Clone by list() method
4. Clone by module

1. Clone by assignment

One list is assigned to another list.

New=original

It creates a new reference to the original list **like aliasing**.

Example 4.28:

```
list1=[1,2]
list2=list1
print("List1 is:",list1)
print("List2 is:",list2)
list1[0]=10
print("List1 is:",list1)
print("List2 is:",list2)
```

Here, list2 is a clone of list1. If any modification is done in one list then it reflects in the other list:

```
List1 is: [1, 2]
List2 is: [1, 2]
List1 is: [10, 2]
List2 is: [10, 2]
```

2. Clone by slicing

Clone is created by using slice operator ([:]).

New=original[:]

[:] operator copies the element in one list from beginning to end into another list. The modification done in one object will not affect the other object.

For example,

```
list1=[1,2]
list2=list1[:]
print("List1 is:",list1)
print("List2 is:",list2)
list1[0]=10
```

```
print("List1 is:",list1)
print("List2 is:",list2)
list2[1]=20
print("List1 is:",list1)
print("List2 is:",list2)
```

Output:

```
List1 is: [1, 2]
List2 is: [1, 2]
List1 is: [10, 2]
List2 is: [1, 2]
List1 is: [10, 2]
List2 is: [1, 20]
```

3. Clone by list() method

The *list* method (refer page no. 4.3) is used to create the clone. This is same as clone by slicing.

Example 4.29:

```
list1=[1,2]
list2=list(list1)
print("List1 is:",list1)
print("List2 is:",list2)
list1[1]=10
print("List1 is:",list1)
print("List2 is:",list2)
list2[1]=20
print("List1 is:",list1)
print("List2 is:",list2)
```

Output:

```
List1 is: [1, 2]
List2 is: [1, 2]
List1 is: [1, 10]
List2 is: [1, 2]
List1 is: [1, 10]
List2 is: [1, 20]
```

Changes made in one object will not affect the other object.

4. Clone by *copy* module

***copy* module** is used to clone an object. There are two copy methods.

1. *copy()*
2. *deepcopy()*

copy() – *copy()* is similar to clone by slice.

Syntax:

```
import copy
new= copy.copy(original)
```

It copies the contents of the original list to the new list.

Example 4.30:

```
import copy
list1=[1,2]
list2=copy.copy(list1)
print("List1 is:",list1)
print("List2 is:",list2)
list1[1]=10
print("List1 is:",list1)
print("List2 is:",list2)
list2[1]=20
print("List1 is:",list1)
print("List2 is:",list2)
```

Output:

```
List1 is: [1, 2]
List2 is: [1, 2]
List1 is: [1, 10]
List2 is: [1, 2]
List1 is: [1, 10]
List2 is: [1, 20]
```

deepcopy() – creates an entirely new list, which has no bindings with the original list. A copy of object is copied in other object. It means any changes made to a copy of object do not reflect in the original object. This method is slower and also consumes more memory.

Syntax:

```
import copy
new= copy.deepcopy(original)
```

Example 4.31:

```
import copy
list1=[10,20,['x','y']]
list2=copy.deepcopy(list1)
print("List1 is:",list1)
print("List2 is:",list2)
list2[0]='a'
list2[2][1]='d'
print("List1 is:",list1)
print("List2 is:",list2)
```

Output:

```
List1 is: [10, 20, ['x', 'y']]
List2 is: [10, 20, ['x', 'y']]
List1 is: [10, 20, ['x', 'y']]
List2 is: ['a', 20, ['x', 'd']]
```

4.1.9 List Parameters

A list can be passed as a parameter to a function.

If changes are done inside the function definition, then it is reflected in the calling program.

The list arguments are always passed by reference only.

Example 4.32:

```
def modify_list(t):
  del t[0]
  t.insert(3,'e')
letter=['a','b','c','d']
print("Before calling:",letter)
modify_list(letter)
print("After calling:",letter)
```

Output:

```
Before calling: ['a', 'b', 'c', 'd']
After calling: ['b', 'c', 'd', 'e']
```

Here, the parameter 't' and the variable 'letter' are aliases for the same object. All the changes done at modify_list function in the list 't', are reflected in the original list 'letter'.

pop() and *remove*() methods can also be used to delete the list elements. It is important to distinguish between the operations that modify the list and that create a new list.

For example, *append*() – modifies a list and '+' operator creates a new list.

Example 4.33:

```
list1=[1,2]
list2=list1.append(3)
print("List1 is:",list1)
print("List2 is:",list2)
list3=list1+[4]
print("List3 is:",list3)
```

Output:

```
List1 is: [1, 2, 3]
List2 is: None
List3 is: [1, 2, 3, 4]
```

4.2 TUPLES

Tuple is a sequence of any type of values separated by comma and enclosed within parentheses. It is similar to lists but it is immutable. It means the tuple cannot be modified.

The differences between the tuple and the list are the tuple cannot be modified like lists and tuple uses parentheses, whereas list uses square brackets.

Example 4.34:

```
fruits=('apple', 'orange')
print(fruits)
```

Output:

```
('apple', 'orange')
```

4.2.1 Creating and accessing tuple

Tuples can be created by putting different values together separated by comma and enclosed within parenthesis.

Syntax:

```
Tuplename=(value1, value2, ..., valueN)
```

To access the tuple elements, slicing operator([]) along with index or indices is used.

There are two type of indexing:

1. Positive indexing / Forward indexing

   Positive indices start from the beginning of the tuple and move towards right.

2. Negative indexing / Backward indexing

   Negative indices start from the end of the tuple and move towards left.

Forward	**0**	**1**	**2**	**3**	**4**	**5**	
	P	**Y**	**T**	**H**	**O**	**N**	
	-6	**-5**	**-4**	**-3**	**-2**	**-1**	**Backward**

Example 4.35:

```
#Tuple Example
t1=(10,20,30)
print("Tuple t1 is:",t1)
#Nested Tuple
t2=("Python",('a','b','c'))
print("Tuple t2 is:",t2)
print("Tuple t2[0] is:",t2[0])
print("Tuple t2[1] is:",t2[1])
print("Tuple t2[1][1] is:",t2[1][1])
#mixed tuple
t3=(3,"aaa")
v1,v2=t3#multiple assignment can be done in tuples
print("Tuple t3 is:",t3)
print("Tuple t3[0] is:",v1)
print("Tuple t3[1] is:",v2)
```

Output:

```
Tuple t1 is: (10, 20, 30)
Tuple t2 is: ('Python', ('a', 'b', 'c'))
Tuple t2[0] is: Python
Tuple t2[1] is: ('a', 'b', 'c')
Tuple t2[1][1] is: b
Tuple t3 is: (3, 'aaa')
Tuple t3[0] is: 3
Tuple t3[1] is: aaa
```

4.2.2 Operations in tuples

Tuple can undergo operations like a string such as concatenation, indexing, slicing, the *len* function etc.

1. Concatenation Operator (+)

'+' Operator is used to join two tuples

Example:

```
t1=(10,20,30)
t2=('aa','bb')
print("Concatenation of t1+t2:",t1+t2)
```

Output:

```
Concatenation of t1+t2: (10, 20, 30, 'aa', 'bb')
```

2. Repetition Operator (*)

'*' operator is used for repetition. It creates a new tuple by repeating the existing tuple the given number of times.

Example:

```
t2=('aa','bb')
print("Repeat the tuple 3 times:",t2*3)
```

Output:

```
Repeat the tuple 3 times: ('aa', 'bb', 'aa', 'bb', 'aa', 'bb')
```

3. Membership Operator (*in*):

The *in* operator is used to test the membership. It returns true if the element is present in a tuple otherwise it returns *False*.

Example 4.36:

```
t1=(1,2,3,4)
print("Tuple t1: ",t1)
print("2 in Tuple t1: ",2 in t1)
print("6 in Tuple t1: ",6 in t1)
```

Output:

```
Tuple t1:  (1, 2, 3, 4)
2 in Tuple t1:  True
6 in Tuple t1:  False
```

4. Inverse Operator (*not in*) or Membership Operator:

The inverse operator *not in* returns *False* if the element is present in a tuple otherwise it returns *True*.

Example 4.37:

```
t1=(1,2,3,4)
print("Tuple t1: ",t1)
```

```
print("2 not in Tuple t1: ",2 not in t1)
print("6 not in Tuple t1: ",6 not in t1)
```

Output:

```
Tuple t1:  (1, 2, 3, 4)
2 not in Tuple t1:  False
6 not in Tuple t1:  True
```

4.2.3 Slicing and indexing of tuples

A subset of elements present in a tuple is called as tuple slice. The operator [m:n] returns the part of the tuple from m^{th} index to n^{th} index, including the element at m^{th} index but excluding the element at n^{th} index.

If the 1st index is omitted then the slice starts at the beginning of the tuple.

If the 2nd index is omitted then the slice goes to the end of the tuple.

If both indices are omitted then the slice is the given tuple itself.

Example 4.38:

```
x =("one", "two", "three", "four")
print("Tuple x is: ",x)
print("x[0]   : ",x[0])
print("x[2]   : ",x[2])
print("x[-1]  : ",x[-1])
print("x[-2]  : ",x[-2])
print("x[1:-1] : ",x[1:-1])
print("x[1:1]  : ",x[1:1])
print("x[4:2]  : ",x[4:2]) #starting index exceeds the length
print("x[0:3]  : ",x[0:3])
print("x[-2:-1]: ",x[-2:-1])
print("x[:3]   : ",x[:3])
```

Output:

```
Tuple x is:  ('one', 'two', 'three', 'four')
x[0]   :  one
x[2]   :  three
x[-1]  :  four
x[-2]  :  three
x[1:-1] :  ('two', 'three')
x[1:1]  :  ()
x[4:2]  :  ()
x[0:3]  :  ('one', 'two', 'three')
```

```
x[-2:-1]:  ('three',)
x[:3]    :  ('one', 'two', 'three')
```

4.2.4 Updating tuples

Tuples are immutable. It means tuple elements cannot be updated or changed. But it is possible to add the portions of existing tuples with new tuple to create another tuple.

Example 4.39:

```
>>> t1=('a','b','c')
>>> t1[0]='A'
Traceback (most recent call last):
  File "<pyshell#8>", line 1, in <module>
    t1[0]='A'
TypeError: 'tuple' object does not support item assignment
>>> t1=('A',)+t1[1:]
>>> print(t1)
('A', 'b', 'c')
```

Here ('A',) is a single element tuple. If there is no comma at the end ('A') then it is considered as a string. The first element 'a' is replaced with 'A'. A new tuple is created with the value 'A' and is combined with the sliced tuple 't1' with the elements from index 1 to the last element.

4.2.5 Deleting tuple elements

Tuples are immutable. So, it is not possible to delete a single element. But it is possible to delete an entire tuple using '*del*' function.

Example 4.40:

```
>>> t1=('a','b','c')
>>> print(t1)
('a', 'b', 'c')
>>> del(t1[0])
Traceback (most recent call last):
  File "<pyshell#17>", line 1, in <module>
    del(t1[0])
TypeError: 'tuple' object doesn't support item deletion
>>> del(t1)
>>> print(t1)
Traceback (most recent call last):
```

```
File "<pyshell#19>", line 1, in <module>
  print(t1)
NameError: name 't1' is not defined
```

4.2.6 Tuple functions

The following functions are used in tuple.

1. *len()*:

len(s) returns the number of elements in a sequence s.

Syntax:

```
len(tuple)
```

Example 4.41:

```
t1=(1,2,3,4)
print("No. of elements in the tuple t1 is:",len(t1))
```

Output:

```
No. of elements in the tuple t1 is: 4
```

2. *max()* & *min()*:

max(s) returns the largest value in a sequence 's' and ***min***(s) returns the smallest value in a sequence 's'

Syntax:

```
max(tuple)
min(tuple)
```

Example 4.42:

```
t1=(10,20,30,40)
print("Maximum value in tuple t1: ",max(t1))
print("Minimum value in tuple t1: ",min(t1))
```

Output:

```
Maximum value in tuple t1:  40
Minimum value in tuple t1:  10
```

3. *tuple()*:

tuple() function is used to convert a sequence (list or string) into tuple.

Syntax:

```
tuple(sequence)
```

where sequence is a string or list.

Example 4.43:

```
s="Python"
list1=[1,2,3,4]
print("String s: ",s)
```

```
print("Convert string into tuple: ",tuple(s))
print("List list1: ",list1)
print("Convert list into tuple : ",tuple(list1))
```

Output:

```
String s:  Python
Convert string into tuple:  ('P', 'y', 't', 'h', 'o', 'n')
List list1:  [1, 2, 3, 4]
Convert list into tuple :  (1, 2, 3, 4)
```

4. *sum()*

sum() function is used to add all the elements in the tuple. Key must be a numeral otherwise it will raise TypeError exception.

Syntax:

```
sum(tuple)
```

Example 4.44:

```
t1 =(1,2,3,4,5,6)
print("Tuple t1:",t1)
print("Sum of tuple t1 is:",sum(t1))
```

Output:

```
Tuple t1: (1, 2, 3, 4, 5, 6)
Sum of tuple t1 is: 21
```

5. *sorted()*

sorted() function is used to sort the tuple in ascending order.

Syntax:

```
sorted(tuple)
```

Example 4.45:

```
t1 =(5,10,6,2,1,7)
print("Tuple t1:",t1)
print("Sorted tuple t1 is:",sorted(t1)) # sorted tuple will be enclosed
#within square brackets
```

Output:

```
Tuple t1: (5, 10, 6, 2, 1, 7)
Sorted tuple t1 is: [1, 2, 5, 6, 7, 10]
```

6. *all()*

all() function returns *True* if all the elements of the tuple are true or empty tuple. Otherwise, it returns *False*.

Syntax:

```
all(tuple)
```

Example 4.46:

```
t1 =(1,2,3,9,0)
print("Tuple t1:",t1)
print("All of t1:",all(t1))
t2 =(1,'0',2,9)
print("Tuple t2:",t2)
print("All of t2:",all(t2))
t3=()
print("Tuple t3:",t3)
print("All of t3:",all(t3))
```

Output:

```
Tuple t1: (1, 2, 3, 9, 0)
All of t1: False
Tuple t2: (1, '0', 2, 9)
All of t2: True
Tuple t3: ()
All of t3: True
```

7. *any()*

any() function returns *True* if any element of the tuple is non-zero. If the tuple is empty or all the elements are zero then it returns *False.*

Syntax:

```
any(tuple)
```

Example 4.47:

```
t1 =(1,2,3,9,0)
print("Tuple t1:",t1)
print("Any of t1:",any(t1))
t2 =(1,'0',2,9)
print("Tuple t2:",t2)
print("Any of t2:",any(t2))
t3=()
print("Tuple t3:",t3)
print("Any of t3:",any(t3))
```

```
t4=(0,0,0)
print("Tuple t4:",t4)
print("Any of t4:",any(t4))
```

Output:

```
Tuple t1: (1, 2, 3, 9, 0)
Any of t1: True
Tuple t2: (1, '0', 2, 9)
Any of t2: True
Tuple t3: ()
Any of t3: False
Tuple t4: (0, 0, 0)
Any of t4: False
```

8. *enumerate()*

***enumerate*()** returns an *enumerate* object. An *enumerate* object contains the index and value of all the items of tuple as pairs.

Example 4.48:

```
t1 =(10,20,30,40,50)
print("index:value")
for i,a in enumerate(t1):
    print(" ",i,":",a)
```

Output:

```
index:value
  0 : 10
  1 : 20
  2 : 30
  3 : 40
  4 : 50
```

4.2.7 Tuple Assignment

Tuple assignment makes it possible to create and assign values for more than one variable in a single statement itself.

Python allows a tuple of variables on the left of an assignment operator and a tuple of values to be assigned on the right of the assignment operator.

The number of variables in left and right sides of the assignment operator must be equal. The right side of the assignment operator can be any kind of data type (string, list or tuple). For example,

```
>>> (a,b,c)=(1,2,3)
```

Left side of an assignment operator is a tuple of variables and right side of an assignment operator is a tuple of values. Each value is assigned to its respective variable.

If the expressions are present on the right side of an assignment operator they are evaluated before any of the assignments.

Two operations are possible:

1. Packing – place values into a new tuple
2. Unpacking – extract those values back into variables.

Example 4.49:

```
>>> t1=("Abi",19,"CSE")# tuple packing
>>> (name,age,branch)=t1# tuple unpacking
>>> print(t1)
('Abi', 19, 'CSE')
>>> print(name)
Abi
>>> print(age)
19
>>> print(branch)
CSE
```

1. Assigning three values using tuple assignment

```
(a,b,c)=(10,20,30)
print("a =",a,"\nb =",b,"\nc =",c)
```

Output:

```
a = 10
b = 20
c = 30
```

2. To generate fibonacci series

```
f1,f2=-1,1
c=1
print("Fibonacci Series")
while(c<=10):
    f1,f2=f2,f1+f2#Multiple assignments f1=f2 and f2=f1+f2
    print(f2)
    c=c+1
```

Output:

```
Fibonacci Series
0
```

```
1
1
2
3
5
8
13
21
34
```

4.2.8 Tuple as return value (Functions can return tuples)

In general a function can return only one value. But it is possible to return more than one value using tuple.

Two integers x and y may be divided and the quotient and the remainder may be computed by using the two operations x/y and x%y separately. But in Python, it is possible to compute both results at the same time by using *divmod* built-in function. d*ivmod* function takes two arguments and returns a tuple of two values as quotient and remainder.

For example,

```
t=divmod(41,3)#returns quoient and remainder
        print(t)
```

Output:

```
(13, 2)
```

Tuple assignment can be used to store the elements separately.

For example,

```
a=int(input("Enter the dividend: "))
b=int(input("Enter the divisor: "))
q,r=divmod(a,b)#returns quotient and remainder
print("Quotient of",a,"/",b," is:",q)
print("Remainder of",a,"%",b," is:",r)
```

Output:

```
Enter the dividend: 41
Enter the divisor: 3
Quotient of 41 / 3  is: 13
Remainder of 41 % 3  is: 2
```

To return the smallest and largest values in a sequence, *min*() and *max*() built-in functions are used.

For example,

```
def minmax(t):
  return(min(t),max(t))
t1=(10,50,20,40)
min,max=minmax(t1)
print("Tuple is:",t1)
print("Minimum tuple value is:",min)
print("Maximum tuple value is:",max)
```

Output:

```
Tuple is: (10, 50, 20, 40)
Minimum tuple value is: 10
Maximum tuple value is: 50
```

Here, minmax is a user-defined function. It computes both minimum and maximum values and returns a tuple of two values.

4.2.9 Variable number of arguments

Sometimes the number of arguments that can be passed into a function is not known in advance. Python allows handling this situation through function call with variable number of arguments or arbitrary number of arguments.

These arguments are received from function definition through single parameter with asterisk (*) before the parameter name. These variable numbers of arguments are collected into tuple.

For example,

```
def employee(*args):
  print(args)
employee("Raja",42,35000,'Pudukkottai')
```

Output:

```
('Raja', 42, 35000, 'Pudukkottai')
```

Here, *employee* is a function definition. *employee* function is called with 4 arguments such as "Raja",42,35000,'Pudukkottai'. These 4 arguments are received through function definition with one parameter *'args'* with * before the parameter name *'args'*. These 4 arguments are collected as tuple and stored in the parameter **args*.

4.3 DICTIONARIES

Dictionary is one of the data types like list. In a list indices are integers but in a dictionary it can be any type. In a dictionary, values are accessed through a key.

A dictionary is a mapping between set of keys (indices) and set of values. Each key maps to one value. The association of a key and a value is known as a key-value pair or an item. All key-value pairs are enclosed within curly braces ({}) and each pair is separated by comma. A key and a value are separated by colon (:). A value can be any data type.

In dictionary the keys are immutable.

A dictionary is a set of zero or more ordered pairs (key, value) such that:

- The value can be any type, may be unique and mutable.
- Each shall occur only once in the dictionary
- Keys must be unique. A key may not be a list or tuple or dictionary.

Dictionaries in Python are implemented using hash table which is an array whose indices are obtained using a hash function on the keys. A hash function takes a key value and returns hash value as an integer. It is used in the dictionary to store and lookup a key-value pair.

Syntax:

Variable={key1:value1, key2:value2,..., keyN:valueN}

4.3.1 Creating dictionary

There are two ways to create dictionaries.

1. A dictionary is created by specifying some or no key-value pairs.
2. *dict*() built-in function is used to create new dictionary with no items.

A dictionary is an unordered object. The order of the key-value pair may be changed arbitrarily after creation. Therefore the values cannot be accessed by specifying their original location like 1st, 2nd, 3rd and so on.

Example 4.50:

```
d1={} #empty dictionary
print(d1)
d2={1:'fruit',2:'vegetables',3:'cereals'} #key as integers and value as strings
print(d2)
d3={'name':'Raja',1:[10,20,30],'rollno':30}#mixed keys
print(d3)
d4=dict() #empty dictionary
print(d4)
```

Output:

```
{}
{1: 'fruit', 2: 'vegetables', 3: 'cereals'}
```

```
{'name': 'Raja', 1: [10, 20, 30], 'rollno': 30}
{}
```

4.3.2 Access, update and add elements in dictionary

1. Access elements

There are two ways to access a value (element) in a dictionary:

1. Using key within square bracket
2. Using *get*() method

The difference is while using *get*() method it returns *None* if the key is not found whereas using key it returns keyError.

For Example,

```
>>> d1={'name':'Raja',1:[10,20,30],'rollno':30}
>>> print(d1[2])
Traceback (most recent call last):
  File "<pyshell#11>", line 1, in <module>
    print(d1[2])
KeyError: 2

>>> print(d1.get(2))
None
```

2. Add and update the elements

Values or items can be added or the value of existing items can be changed in a dictionary. If the key is present then its value gets updated otherwise a new key-value pair is added to the dictionary.

For Example,

```
d1={} #empty dictionary
d1['1']="Monday"
d1['2']="Tuesday"
d1['3']="Wednesday"
print("Dictionary d1:",d1)
print("Display the key value 3:",d1['3'])
d2={'name':'Krishnan','age':30}
print("Dictionary d2:",d2)
print("Display the value of age:",d2['age'])
d2['age']=35#Update existing key
d2['location']='Trichy'#Add new key 'location'
print("After the updation of d2:",d2)
```

Output:

```
Dictionary d1: {'1': 'Monday', '2': 'Tuesday', '3': 'Wednesday'}
Display the key value 3: Wednesday
Dictionary d2: {'name': 'Krishnan', 'age': 30}
Display the value of age: 30
After the updation of d2: {'name': 'Krishnan', 'age': 35, 'location':
'Trichy'}
```

4.3.3 Deletion of elements

An element in the dictionary can be deleted by using *del* statement.

The entire dictionary can be deleted by using *del* statement with the dictionary variable name.

A particular item in a dictionary can be removed by using the method *pop* (). This method removes the item with the provided key and returns the value.

The method *popitem* () can be used to remove and return the current last item (key, value) from the dictionary.

All items can be removed at once using *clear* () method.

For Example,

```
cube={1:1,2:8,3:27,4:64,5:125,6:216}
print("Dictionary cube is:", cube)
print("Pop of 4 returns:",cube.pop(4))#delete the key 4
print("After pop operation the dictionary cube is:", cube)
print(cube.popitem())#removes the last key-value pair
print("After popitem operation:", cube)
del(cube[1])#delete the key 1
print("After deleting the key 1:",cube)
cube.clear()#delete all key-value pairs
print("Display Empty Dictionary:", cube)
del cube#delete the dictionary cube
print(cube)
```

Output:

```
Dictionary cube is: {1: 1, 2: 8, 3: 27, 4: 64, 5: 125, 6: 216}
Pop of 4 returns: 64
After pop operation the dictionary cube is: {1: 1, 2: 8, 3: 27, 5: 125, 6:
216}
(6, 216)
After popitem operation: {1: 1, 2: 8, 3: 27, 5: 125}
```

```
After deleting the key 1: {2: 8, 3: 27, 5: 125}
Display Empty Dictionary: {}
Traceback (most recent call last):
  File "C:/Python/Python37-32/d3.py", line 12, in <module>
    print(cube)
NameError: name 'cube' is not defined
```

4.3.4 Dictionary methods

The methods are accessed as **dictionary variable. method name()**

1. ***clear()***

clear() method removes all elements from the dictionary. It does not return any value and also does not take any arguments.

Syntax:

```
dictionaryname.clear()
```

Example 4.51:

```
squares={1:1,2:4,3:9,4:16,5:25}
print("Before clear() method the dictionary is:",squares)
squares.clear()#delete all key-value pairs
print("After clear() method the dictionary squares is
empty:",squares)
```

Output:

```
Before clear() method the dictionary is: {1: 1, 2: 4, 3: 9, 4: 16,
5: 25}
After clear() method the dictionary squares is empty: {}
```

2. ***copy()***

copy() method returns a copy of the dictionary. It doesn't take any arguments.

Syntax:

```
dictionaryname.copy()
```

If any change is done in the duplicate copy of the dictionary it does not reflect in the original dictionary and vice versa.

Example 4.52:

```
squares={1:1,2:4,3:9,4:16,5:25}
new=squares.copy()
print("The dictionary squares is:",squares)
print("The dictionary new is:",new)
del new[3]
```

```
print("After deleting the key 3 in new dictionary:")
print("The dictionary squares is:",squares)
print("The dictionary new is:",new)
```

Output:

```
The dictionary squares is: {1: 1, 2: 4, 3: 9, 4: 16, 5: 25}
The dictionary new is: {1: 1, 2: 4, 3: 9, 4: 16, 5: 25}
After deleting the key 3 in new dictionary:
The dictionary squares is: {1: 1, 2: 4, 3: 9, 4: 16, 5: 25}
The dictionary new is: {1: 1, 2: 4, 4: 16, 5: 25}
```

Deleting the key 3 in *new* dictionary did not affect the original dictionary.

3. *fromkeys()*

fromkeys() method creates a new dictionary from the given sequence of keys with an optional value provided by the user.

Syntax:

```
dictionaryname.fromkeys(sequence[,value])
```

where 'value' is optional.

Example 4.53:

```
keys={'one','two','three','four'}
d1=dict.fromkeys(keys)#without value
print("The dictionary d1:",d1)
d2=dict.fromkeys(keys,1)#with value 1
print("The dictionary d2:",d2)
```

Output:

```
The dictionary d1: {'four': None, 'three': None, 'one': None,
'two': None}
The dictionary d2: {'four': 1, 'three': 1, 'one': 1, 'two': 1}
```

(Note: It may be noted in the above output that the order of the key-value pairs is changed. The order may not remain the same any time.)

4. *get()*

get() method returns the value for the specified key, if the key is present in dictionary.

Syntax:

```
dictionaryname.get (keys[,value])
```

where 'value' is optional. The *get()* method returns

- *None*, if the key is not found and value is not specified
- value, if the key is not found and value is specified.

Example 4.54:

```
d1={'name':'Mary','age':41}
print("Dictionary d1 is:",d1)
print("Name:",d1.get('name'))
print("Age :",d1.get('age'))
print("Salary:",d1.get('salary'))#without value
print("Salary:",d1.get('salary',20000))#with value
```

Output:

```
Dictionary d1 is: {'name': 'Mary', 'age': 41}
Name: Mary
Age : 41
Salary: None
Salary: 20000
```

Here, the key 'salary' is not available in the dictionary d1. If we use d1.get('salary'), it returns the value *None*. If we use d1.get('salary',20000), it returns the value 20000 even though the key:value pair is not present in the dictionary.

5. ***items()***

items() method returns a view object that displays a list of all the dictionary key-value pairs in tuple form. It does not take any arguments. A view object is one which displays the content and no operations on them are possible.

Syntax:

```
dictionaryname.items()
```

Example 4.55:

```
d1={1:'Monday',2:'Tuesday',3:'Wednesday',4:'Thursday'}
print(d1.items())
```

Output:

```
dict_items([(1, 'Monday'), (2, 'Tuesday'), (3, 'Wednesday'), (4,
'Thursday')])
```

6. ***keys()***

keys() method returns a view object that displays a list of all the keys in dictionary. It does not take any arguments.

Syntax:

```
dictionaryname.keys()
```

Example 4.56:

```
d1={1:'Monday',2:'Tuesday',3:'Wednesday',4:'Thursday'}
print(d1.keys())
```

```
d2={}
print(d2.keys())
```

Output:

```
dict_keys([1, 2, 3, 4])
dict_keys([])
```

7. ***pop()***

pop() method returns the value that is removed from the dictionary with the specified key.

Syntax:

```
dictionaryname.pop(key[,default])
```

The pop() method takes two arguments:

1. key – which is to be searched for removal
2. default – value to be returned when the key is not in the dictionary

The pop() method returns:

1. If the key is found then it returns the corresponding value
2. If the key is not found then it returns the default value if specified in the pop method.
3. If the key is not found and the default value is not specified in the pop method then it will raise a KeyError exception.

Example 4.57:

```
d1={1:'one',2:'two',3:'three',4:'four',5:'five'}
print("Dictionary d1 is:",d1)
print("Pop of 4 returns:",d1.pop(4))
print("After pop(4) the dictionary d1 is:",d1)
print("Pop of 6 returns:",d1.pop(6,'six'))#default value is six
print("Pop of 7 returns:",d1.pop(7))#No defaultvalue; Raise a
KeyError Exception
```

Output:

```
Dictionary d1 is: {1: 'one', 2: 'two', 3: 'three', 4: 'four', 5: 'five'}
Pop of 4 returns: four
After pop(4) the dictionary d1 is: {1: 'one', 2: 'two', 3: 'three', 5:
'five'}
Pop of 6 returns: six
Traceback (most recent call last):
  File "C:/Python/Python37-32/d10.py", line 5, in <module>
    print("Pop of 7 returns:",d1.pop(7))#No defaultvalue; Raise a
KeyError Exception
KeyError: 7
```

8. *popitem()*

popitem() returns and removes the current last item(key:value pair) from the dictionary. It does not take any arguments.

Syntax:

```
dictionaryname.popitem()
```

Example 4.58:

```
d1={'apple':25,'orange':20,'lemon':5,'Guava':10}
print("Dictionary d1 is:",d1)
print("Popitem returns:",d1.popitem())
print("After popitem method the dictionary d1 is:",d1)
```

Output:

```
Dictionary d1 is: {'apple': 25, 'orange': 20, 'lemon': 5, 'Guava': 10}
Popitem returns: ('Guava', 10)
After popitem method the dictionary d1 is: {'apple': 25, 'orange': 20, 'lemon': 5}
```

9. *setdefault()*

setdefault() method returns the value of a key if the key is in the dictionary. If the key is not in the dictionary then it inserts the key with value in the dictionary.

Syntax:

```
dictionaryname.setdefault(key[,default-value])
```

The setdefault() method takes two arguments:

1. key – which is to be searched in the dictionary
2. default-value(optional) – key with default value is inserted in the dictionary, if the key is not in the dictionary; If there is no value then default is *None.*

The setdefault () method returns:

1. *None* - if the key is not found and the default value is not specified
2. default-value - if the key is not found and the default value is specified

Example 4.59:

```
d1={'name':'Raja','age':40}
print("Dictionary d1 is:",d1)
print("setdefault of age returns:",d1.setdefault('age'))
print("setdefault of name returns:",d1.setdefault('name','ss'))
```

```
print("setdefault of location
returns:",d1.setdefault('location','Villupuram'))
print("Dictionary d1 is:",d1)
```

Output:

```
Dictionary d1 is: {'name': 'Raja', 'age': 40}
setdefault of age returns: 40
setdefault of name returns: Raja
setdefault of location returns: Villupuram
Dictionary d1 is: {'name': 'Raja', 'age': 40, 'location':
'Villupuram'}
```

Note the statement **d1.setdefault('name','ss')** – as the key 'name' is in dictionary d1and it returns the corresponding value 'Raja'. The default value 'ss' is not used.

10.*update*()

***update*()** method updates the dictionary with the key-value pair of another dictionary object. The update() method adds key-value pair to the dictionary, if the key is not in the dictionary. If the key is in the dictionary then it updates the key with new value.

Syntax:

```
Dictionaryname1.update(dictionaryname2)
```

Example 4.60:

```
d1={1:'Monday',2:'Wednesday'}
d2={2:'Tuesday'}
print("Before update the dictionary d1 is:",d1)
d1.update(d2)#update the value of key 2
print("After update the dictionary d1 is:",d1)
d3={3:'Wednesday'}
d1.update(d3)#add a new key-value pair
print("After update(add) the dictionary d1 is:",d1)
```

Output:

```
Before update the dictionary d1 is: {1: 'Monday', 2:
'Wednesday'}
After update the dictionary d1 is: {1: 'Monday', 2: 'Tuesday'}
After update(add) the dictionary d1 is: {1: 'Monday', 2:
'Tuesday', 3: 'Wednesday'}
```

11. ***values()***

values() method returns a view object that displays a list of all the values in dictionary. It does not take any arguments.

Syntax:

```
dictionaryname.values()
```

Example 4.61:

```
d1={1:'Monday',2:'Tuesday',3:'Wednesday',4:'Thursday'}
print(d1.values())
d2={}
print(d2.values())
```

Output:

```
dict_values(['Monday', 'Tuesday', 'Wednesday', 'Thursday'])
dict_values([])
```

4.3.5 Dictionary functions

The following functions are used in dictionary.

1. ***len():***

len() returns the number of key-value pairs in a dictionary.

Syntax:

```
len(dictionaryname)
```

Example 4.62:

```
d1={1:'Monday',2:'Tuesday',3:'Wednesday',4:'Thursday'}
print("No. of elements in the dictionary d1 is:",len(d1))
```

Output:

```
No. of elements in the dictionary d1 is: 4
```

2. ***max() & min():***

max() returns the largest key in a dictionary and ***min***() returns the smallest key in a dictionary.

Syntax:

```
max(dictionaryname)
min(dictionaryname)
```

Example 4.63:

```
d1={1:'Monday',2:'Tuesday',3:'Wednesday',4:'Thursday'}
print("Largest key in the dictionary d1: ",max(d1))
print("Smallest key in the dictionary d1: ",min(d1))
```

Output:

```
Largest key in the dictionary d1:  4
Smallest key in the dictionary d1:  1
```

3. *sum()*

sum() function is used to add all the keys in the dictionary. Key must be a numeral otherwise it will raise TypeError exception.

Syntax:

sum(dictionaryname)

Example 4.64:

```
d1={1:10,2:20,3:30,4:40}
print("Sum of d1: ",sum(d1))#sum the keys
d1={1.0:10,2.0:20,3.0:30,4.0:40}
print("Sum of d1: ",sum(d1))#sum the keys
d1={'1':10,'2':20,'3':30,'4':40}
print("Sum of d1: ",sum(d1))#TypeError Exception
```

Output:

```
Sum of d1:  10
Sum of d1:  10.0
Traceback (most recent call last):
  File "C:/Python/Python37-32/d16.py", line 6, in <module>
    print("Sum of d1: ",sum(d1))#TypeError Exception
TypeError: unsupported operand type(s) for +: 'int' and 'str'
```

4. *sorted()*

sorted() function is used to sort the dictionary in order based on key.

Syntax:

sorted(dictionary[,reverse])

where *reverse* is optional. If *reverse* is *True* then it displays the key in descending order otherwise in ascending order. Default of reverse is *False*.

Example 4.65:

```
d1={'e':2,'u':5,'a':1,'o':4,'i':3}
print("Sorted d1: ",sorted(d1))
print("Reverse order of d1: ",sorted(d1,reverse=True))
```

Output:

```
Sorted d1:  ['a', 'e', 'i', 'o', 'u']
Reverse order of d1:  ['u', 'o', 'i', 'e', 'a']
```

5. *all()*

all() function returns *True* if all the keys of the dictionary are non-zero, or *True,* or if the dictionary is empty. Otherwise, it returns *False.*

Syntax:

```
all(dictionaryname)
```

Example 4.66:

```
d1={'a':1,'e':2,'i':3,'o':4,0:5}
print("Dictionary d1:",d1)
print("All of d1:",all(d1))
d2={False:1,'e':2,'i':3,'o':4,'u':5}
print("Dictionary d2:",d2)
print("All of d2:",all(d2))
d3={}
print("Dictionary d3:",d3)
print("All of d3:",all(d3))
d4={'a':1,'e':2,'i':3,'o':4,'0':False}
print("Dictionary d4:",d4)
print("All of d4:",all(d4))
```

Output:

```
Dictionary d1: {'a': 1, 'e': 2, 'i': 3, 'o': 4, 0: 5}
All of d1: False
Dictionary d2: {False: 1, 'e': 2, 'i': 3, 'o': 4, 'u': 5}
All of d2: False
Dictionary d3: {}
All of d3: True
Dictionary d4: {'a': 1, 'e': 2, 'i': 3, 'o': 4, '0': False}
All of d4: True
```

6. *any()*

any() function returns *True* if any key of the dictionary is non-zero or *True*. If the dictionary is empty or all the keys are zero/*False* then it returns *False*.

Syntax:

```
any(dictionaryname)
```

Example 4.67:

```
d1={'a':1,'e':2,'i':3,'o':4,0:5}
print("Any of d1:",any(d1))
d2={False:1,False:2,False:3,False:4,0:True}
print("Any of d2:",any(d2))
```

```
d3={}
print("Any of d3:",any(d3))
d4={0:1,0:2,0:3,0:4,0:5}
print("Any of d4:",any(d4))
```

Output:

```
Any of d1: True
Any of d2: False
Any of d3: False
Any of d4: False
```

4.4 ADVANCED LIST PROCESSING: LIST COMPREHENSION

List comprehension is a construction that allows sequences to be built from other sequences. It provides a concise way to create a list. It creates a new list in which each element is the result of applying a given operation to a value from a sequence (e.g., the elements in another list).

Syntax:

Newlist=[expression *for* item in list [*if* condition]]

This is equivalent to:

```
for item in list:
    if condition:
        expression
```

A list comprehension consists of the following parts:

- An input sequence
- Variable representing members of the input sequence
- An optional predicate expression
- An output expression producing elements of the output list from the members of the input sequence that satisfy the predicate

Example 4.68:

```
list1=[a**3 for a in range(1,6)]
print(list1)
```

Output:

```
[1, 8, 27, 64, 125]
```

Example 4.69:

```
mixed=[1,2,'x',3.0,4]
print([a**3 for a in mixed if type(a)==int]) #a**3 - output expression, mixed
- input #sequence, if type(a)==int - optional predicate
```

Output:

```
[1, 8, 64]
```

The iterator part iterates through each member 'a' of the input sequence 'mixed'. The predicate checks if the member is an integer. If the member is an integer then it is passed to the output expression, and cubed to become a member of the output list.

Example 4.70:

```
list1=[a**3 for a in [1,2,3]]
print(list1)
list2=[a**3 for a in range(5)]
print(list2)
list3=[ord(ch) for ch in "Welcome"]
print(list3)
list4=[-5,3,-7,-1,6,2,-8,0]
list5=[a for a in list4 if a>=0]
print(list5)
list6=["banana","orange","apple"]
list7=[a[0] for a in list6]
print(list7)
list8=[a*b for a in[1,2,3] for b in[1,2,3]]
print(list8)
```

Output:

```
[1, 8, 27]
[0, 1, 8, 27, 64]
[87, 101, 108, 99, 111, 109, 101]
[3, 6, 2, 0]
['b', 'o', 'a']
[1, 2, 3, 2, 4, 6, 3, 6, 9]
```

4.5 ILLUSTRATIVE PROBLEMS:

Sorting:

Sorting is the process of arranging the elements in a list either in ascending or descending order.

Types of sorting:

- Selection sort
- Insertion sort
- Merge sort
- Quick sort

4.5.1 Selection sort:

During the 1st pass, find the smallest element in the list and swap it with first element. After the 1st pass, the smallest element is in its correct (first) position. Then start the 2nd pass with the second element in the list and find the second smallest element in the list and swap it with 2nd element. Continue this process until the end of the list.

For example,

[34, 67, 12, 89, 26]

1st pass: [12, 67, 34, 89, 26] – 34 and 12 are swapped; 12 is in correct position
2nd pass: [12, 26, 34, 89, 67] – 67 and 26 are swapped; 26 is in correct position
3rd pass: [12, 26, 34, 89, 67] – No swapping; 34 is in correct position
4th pass: [12, 26, 34, 67, 89] – 89 and 67 are swapped; 67 is in correct position
5th pass: [12, 26, 34, 67, 89]

Program:

```
#Function selectionsort defined
def selectionsort(list1):
  for i in range(len(list1)):
    min=i
    for j in range(i+1,len(list1)):
      if list1[j]<list1[min]:
        min=j
    list1[i],list1[min]=list1[min],list1[i]
#Main program segment
n=int(input("Enter the number of elements:"))
a=[]
for i in range(n):
  print("Enter the element ",i)
  x=int(input())
  a.append(x)
print("Given List:",a)
selectionsort(a)
print("Sorted List:",a)
```

Output:

```
Enter the number of elements:5
Enter the element  0
34
```

```
Enter the element 1
67
Enter the element 2
12
Enter the element 3
89
Enter the element 4
26
Given List: [34, 67, 12, 89, 26]
Sorted List: [12, 26, 34, 67, 89]
```

4.5.2 Insertion sort:

The 1st element of the list is assumed to be in correct position. Take the 2nd element and compare with the 1st element. If the 1st element is greater than the 2nd element then the second element is placed in front of the 1st element. Now, the first 2 elements are sorted. Take the 3rd element and compare it with the previous two elements and place it in the correct position. This process is repeated until the end of the list.

For example,

[34, 67, 12, 89, 26]

1st pass: [34, 67, 12, 89, 26] - 67 and 34 are compared and 67 is in correct position

2nd pass: [12, 34, 67, 89, 26] - 12 is compared with 34 and 67 and it is placed in the first position

3rd pass: [12, 34, 67, 89, 26] - 89 is compared with 12, 34 and 67 and it is in correct position

4th pass: [12, 26, 34, 67, 89] - 26 is compared with 12, 34, 67 and 89; it is inserted in its position

Program:

```
#Function insertionsort defined
def insertionsort(list1):
  for i in range(1,len(list1)):
    temp=list1[i]
    j=i
    while j>0 and temp<list1[j-1]:
      list1[j]=list1[j-1]
      j=j-1
```

```
        list1[j]=temp
#Main program segment
n=int(input("Enter the number of elements:"))
a=[]
for i in range(n):
    print("Enter the element ",i)
    x=int(input())
    a.append(x)
print("Given List:",a)
insertionsort(a)
print("Sorted List:",a)
```

Output:

```
Enter the number of elements:5
Enter the element  0
34
Enter the element  1
67
Enter the element  2
12
Enter the element  3
89
Enter the element  4
26
Given List: [34, 67, 12, 89, 26]
Sorted List: [12, 26, 34, 67, 89]
```

4.5.3 Merge Sort:

Merge sort uses divide-and-conquer technique. Merge sort divides a list into several sub-lists repeatedly until each sub-list contains a single element and merges those sub-lists repeatedly that results into a sorted list.

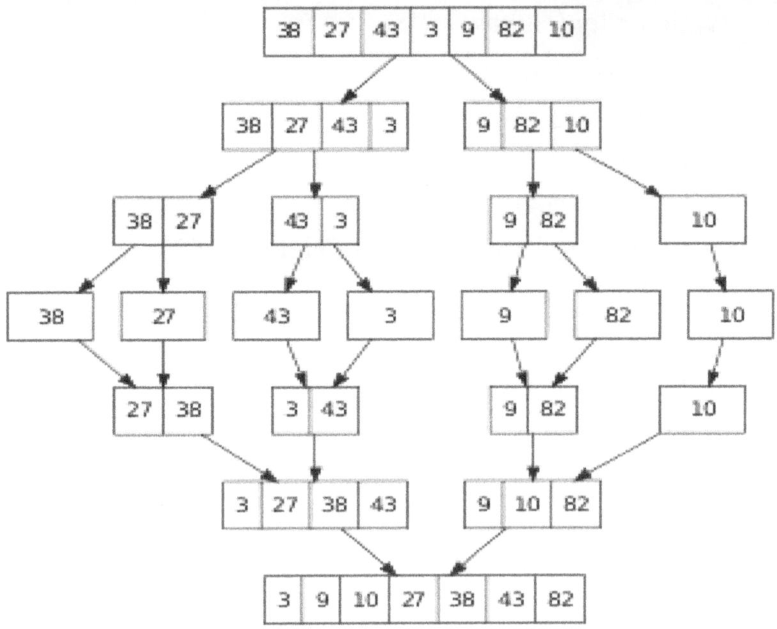

Program:

```
#Function mergesort defined
def mergesort(a):
  if len(a) > 1:
    mid=len(a)//2
    left=a[:mid]
    right=a[mid:]
    mergesort(left)
    mergesort(right)
    i,j,k=0,0,0;
    while i < len(left) and j<len(right):
      if left[i]<right[j]:
        a[k] = left[i]
        i=i+1
      else:
        a[k] = right[j]
        j=j+1
      k=k+1
    while i < len(left):
      a[k] = left[i]
      i=i+1
      k=k+1
```

```
            while j < len(right):
                a[k] = right[j]
                j=j+1
                k=k+1
    #Main program segment
    n=int(input("Enter the number of elements:"))
    a=[]
    for i in range(n):
        print("Enter the element ",i)
        x=int(input())
        a.append(x)
    print("Given List:",a)
    mergesort(a)
    print("Sorted List:",a)
```

Output:

```
Enter the number of elements:7
Enter the element  0
38
Enter the element  1
27
Enter the element  2
43
Enter the element  3
3
Enter the element  4
9
Enter the element  5
82
Enter the element  6
10
Given List: [38, 27, 43, 3, 9, 82, 10]
Sorted List: [3, 9, 10, 27, 38, 43, 82]
```

4.5.4 Histogram

Histogram is a table that shows the frequency of data items.

a) Lookup:

Lookup is a dictionary operation that takes a key and finds its corresponding value.

Example:

```
def histogram(s):
  d=dict()
  for i in s:
    if i in d:
      d[i]+=1
    else:
      d[i]=1
  return d
h=histogram('malayalam')
print(h)
print(h.get('a'))
```

Key	Value
m	2
a	4
l	2
y	1

Output:

```
{'m': 2, 'a': 4, 'l': 2, 'y': 1}
4
```

b) Reverse Lookup:

Reverse Lookup is a dictionary operation that takes a value and finds one or more keys that map to it.

Example:

```
def revl(d,v):
  for i in d:
    if d[i]==v:
      return i
h={'m':2,'a':4,'l':2,'y':1}
print(revl(h,2))
```

Output:

```
m
```

Short Questions

1. What is a list?

A list is a sequence of values. These values are separated by commas and enclosed within square brackets ([ ]). The values can be of any type such as strings, tuples, lists, dictionaries, functions, file objects, and any type of number. A list can be indexed from its front (0, 1, 2, ...) or from back (-1, -2, - 3, ...). Lists are mutable.

2. Solve a) [0] * 4 and b) [1, 2, 3] * 3.

```
>>> [0] * 4
[0, 0, 0, 0]
>>> [1, 2, 3] * 3
[1, 2, 3, 1, 2, 3, 1, 2, 3]
```

3. Let list = ['a', 'b', 'c', 'd', 'e', 'f']. Find a) list[1:3] b) list[:4] c) list [3:] .

```
>>> list = ['a', 'b', 'c', 'd', 'e', 'f']
>>> list[1:3]
['b', 'c']
>>> list[:4]
['a', 'b', 'c', 'd']
>>> list[3:]
['d', 'e', 'f']
```

4. Mention any 5 list methods.

append(), extend (), sort(), pop(), index(), insert() and remove()

5. State the difference between lists and dictionary.

List is a mutable type, that is, its contents can be modified whereas in a dictionary the key is immutable but the value is mutable.

Dictionary is not ordered and it requires that the keys are hashable whereas the list can store a sequence of objects in certain order.

6. What is List mutability in Python? Give an example.

List is a mutable type, that is, its contents can be modified.

Example:

```
>>> list = [17, 123]
>>> list [1] = 5
>>> print(list)
[17, 5]
```

7. What is aliasing in list? Give an example.

When two identifiers are made to refer to the same variable or value, then it is called as aliasing.

For example,

```
>>>list1=[1,2]
>>>list2= list1
>>>print(list1 is list2)
True
```

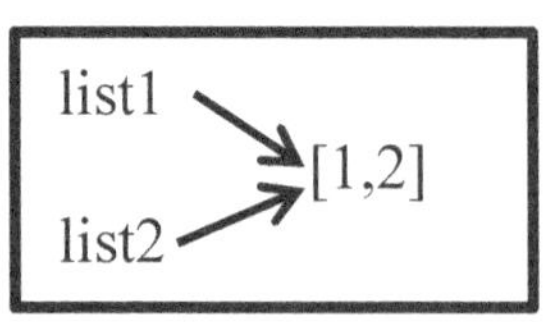

8. Define cloning in list.

Cloning means creating a replica of the original list. It is a process of making a copy of the list without modifying the original list.

When changes are done in the cloning list they will not affect the original list.

9. Explain List parameters with an example.

Passing a list as an argument in a function call actually passes a reference to the list, not a copy of the list. If changes are done in the function definition, then it is reflected in the calling program.

Example:

```
def modify_list(t):
  t.insert(4,'e')
letter=['a','b','c','d']
print("Before calling:",letter)
modify_list(letter)
print("After calling:",letter)
```

Output:

```
Before calling: ['a', 'b', 'c', 'd']
After calling: ['a','b', 'c', 'd', 'e']
```

10. Write a program in Python to delete the first element from a list.

Example:

```
def delete_first_element(t):
  del t[0]
list=['a','b','c','d']
print("Before calling:",list)
delete_first_element(list)
print("After calling:",list)
```

Output:

```
Before calling: ['a', 'b', 'c', 'd']
After calling: ['b', 'c', 'd']
```

11. Write a program in Python to return a list that contains all except the first element of the given list.

```
def tail(list):
   return list[1:]
numbers = [1, 2, 3]
rest = tail(numbers)
print(rest)
```

Output:

```
[2, 3]
```

12. What is the benefit of using tuple assignment in Python?

Tuple assignment is often useful to swap the values of more than one variable without using temporary variable.

```
>>> a, b = (b, a)
```

13. Define key-value pairs.

A dictionary is a mapping between a set of keys (indices) and a set of values. Each key maps to one value. The association of a key and a value is known as a key-value pair or an item.

14. Define dictionary with an example.

A dictionary is a mapping between a set of keys (indices) and a set of values. Each key maps to one value. The association of a key and a value is known as a key-value pair or an item. All key-value pairs are enclosed within curly braces ({}) and each pair is separated by comma. A key and a value are separated by colon (:). A value can be any data type. In dictionary the keys are immutable.

A dictionary is a set of zero or more ordered pairs (key, value) such that:
The value can be any type, may be unique and mutable.
Each key may occur only once in the dictionary
Keys must be unique. A key may not be a list or tuple or dictionary.

Example:

```
d1={} #empty dictionary
print(d1)
d2={1:'fruit',2:'vegetables',3:'cereals'} #key as integers and value as strings
print(d2)
```

Output:

```
{}
{1: 'fruit', 2: 'vegetables', 3: 'cereals'}
```

15. How to return tuples as values?

In general a function can return only one value. But it is possible to return more than one value using tuple.

Two integers x and y may be divided and the quotient and the remainder may be computed by using the two operations x/y and x%y separately. But in Python, it is possible to compute both values at the same time by using *divmod* built-in function. *divmod* function takes two arguments and returns a tuple of two values as quotient and remainder.

For example,

```
t=divmod(7,2)#returns quotient and remainder
print(t)
```

Output:

```
(3, 1)
```

16. Explain two dictionary operations with an example

i. *del* - removes key-value pairs from a dictionary

```
ex: >>> d={1:'M',2:'T',3:'W'}
>>> del d[2]
>>> print(d)
{1: 'M', 3: 'W'}
```

ii. *len* - returns the number of key-value pairs

```
ex: >>> d={1:'M',2:'T',3:'W'}
>>> print(len(d))
3
```

17. Write a Python program to swap two variables x=5 and y=10 without using tuple.

```
x = 5
y = 10
temp = x
x = y
y = temp
print('The value of x after swapping: {}'.format(x))
print('The value of y after swapping: {}'.format(y))
```

18. Write a Python program to swap two values using tuple assignment

```
a=10
b=20
(a,b)=(b,a)
print(a,b)
Output:
20 10
```

19. Define List Comprehension.

List comprehension is a construction that allows sequences to be built from other sequences. It provides a concise way to create a list. It creates a new list in which each element is the result of applying a given operation to a value from a sequence (eg. the elements in another list).

20. Write the syntax for list comprehension and give an example.

Syntax:

Newlist=[expression *for* item *in* list [*if* condition]]

This is equivalent to:

for item in list:

```
if condition:
        expression
```

Example:

```
ist1=[a**3 for a in range(1,6)]
print(list1)
```

Output:

```
[1, 8, 27, 64, 125]
```

Unsolved Exercises

1. Write a Python program to sum all the items in a list.
2. Write a Python program to find the largest number and the smallest number from a list.
3. Write a Python program to get a list sorted in increasing order by the last element in each tuple from a given list of non-empty tuples. Sample list:[(2,5),(1,2),(4,4),(2,3),(2,1)] Expected output: [(2,1),(1,2),(2,3),(4,4),(2,5)]
4. Write a function called *is_sorted* that takes a list as a parameter and returns *True* if the list is sorted in ascending order and *False* otherwise. You can assume (as a precondition) that the elements of the list can be compared using the relational operators <, >, etc.

   For example, *is_sorted* ([2,3,4]) should return *True* and *is_sorted*(['y','x'] should return *False*.
5. Two words are anagrams if you can rearrange the letters from one to spell the other. Write a function called *is_anagram* that takes two strings and returns *True* if they are anagrams.
6. Write a function called *remove_duplicates* that takes a list and returns a new list with only the unique elements from the original. .
7. Write a Python program to add an item in a tuple.
8. Write a Python program to convert a tuple to a string.
9. Write a Python program to find the repeated items of a tuple.
10. Write a Python program to check whether an element exists within a tuple.
11. Write a Python program to unzip a list of tuples into individual lists.
12. Write a Python script to sort a dictionary by value.
13. Write a Python script to concatenate two dictionaries to create a new one.
14. Write a Python script to generate and print a dictionary that contains a number (between 1 and n) in the form (x:x*x). Example: for n=4, expected output: {1:1,2:4,3:9}
15. Write a Python script to map two lists into a dictionary.

UNIT V
FILES, MODULES, PACKAGES

Contents

Files and exception: text files, reading and writing files, format operator, command line arguments, errors and exceptions, handling exceptions, modules, packages; Illustrative programs: word count, copy file

5.1 FILES

A collection of information stored in a location on disk is known as a file. This location is referred with file name.

There are two types of files:

1. Text File
2. Binary File

Text file is formed with a sequence of lines. Each line includes a sequence of words. Each word has a sequence of characters. Each line is terminated with a special character, called EOL (End of Line) character.

Binary file is a file stored in binary format i.e., in the form of bits not in the form of textual information. A binary file is readable by computer. Some special applications are required to read a data stored in a binary file. For example, image file (in bits) is read using image viewer, audio file (in bits) is read using media player.

5.1.1 File Operations

The following operations are performed on text files:

1. Opening a file
2. Reading the contents of a file
3. Writing the data into the file
4. Closing the file

1. Opening a File

Before reading the contents of a file, the file must be opened and the mode of operation must be specified. Mode means what operation is to be performed on the file (read, append, etc.). The file is opened using the built-in function *open*(). The function *open*() creates a file object. This file object is used to support the methods related to file.

Syntax:

File_object_name = *open*("file name"[,mode])

Where,

- file name: The file name is the name of the file that is stored
- mode: The mode argument determines for what operation the file has to be opened, i.e., read, write, append, etc. A complete list of possible mode operations is given in the table below. This is an optional argument and the default mode is read (r).

The list of different modes for opening a file:

Modes	Description
r	A file is opened for read-only mode. The file pointer (file position) is placed at the beginning of the file. This mode is the default mode.
w	A file is opened for write-only mode. If the file already exists then the existing contents are overwritten. Otherwise, a new file is created for writing.
X	A file is opened for exclusive creation mode. If the file already exists then the operation fails.
a	A file is opened for appending mode. If the file already exists then the file pointer is at the end of the file. If the file does not exist then it creates a new file for writing.
r+	A file is opened for both reading and writing mode. The file pointer is placed at the beginning of the file.
w+	A file is opened for both writing and reading mode.
a+	A file is opened for both appending and reading mode.
T	A file is opened in text mode. This is the default mode.
B	A file is opened in binary mode.
rb	Opens a file for read only mode in binary format. The file pointer is placed at the beginning of the file. This is the default mode.
rb+	Opens a file for both read and write mode in binary format. The file pointer is placed at the beginning of the file.
wb	Opens a file for write only mode in binary format.
wb+	Opens a file for both write and read mode in binary format.
ab	Opens a file for append mode in binary format.
ab+	Opens a file for both append and read mode in binary format.

For Example, to open a text file in read-only mode:

```
fp=open('d:\sample.txt', mode='r')
(or)
fp=open('d:\sample.txt', 'r')
```

5.2 READING AND WRITING FILES

5.2.1 Reading a File

For reading the data from a file, first the file is opened in 'r' mode. Then the file method *read* () is used to read the contents of the file. File pointer is at the starting of the file. If the file does not exist then Python raises the exception File Not Found Error.

Syntax:

Fileobject.*read*()

For Example,

```
filename=input("Enter the file name:")
fp=open(filename, 'r')#fp is file pointer
print(fp.read())
```

Output

```
Enter the file name:d:\sample.txt
Welcome to Python Programming
```

File name is either obtained from the user during runtime or explicitly specified in the *open*() function.

Methods used in reading a file:

1. Size of data()
2. tell() and seek()
3. readline()
4. readlines()

1. Using size of data:

Syntax:

Fileobject.*read*([size])

Where, 'size' is an optional argument. 'size' is the number of bytes to be read. If the 'size' is specified then it reads the specified number of bytes. Otherwise it reads an entire file.

Example 5.1:

 # Let sample.txt contain "Welcome to Python Programming"

```
>>> fp=open('d:\sample.txt', 'r')
>>> fp.read()#After read the pointer will be at the end
'Welcome to Python Programming'
```

```
>>> fp.read(1)#There is no character to be read after end
''
>>> fp.close()
>>> fp=open('d:\sample.txt','r')#file pointer will be at the starting of the
    #file
>>> fp.read(10)# First 10 characters will be read
    #'Welcome to'
```

2. tell() & seek() :

a) *tell*() method returns the current file position.

Syntax:

Fileobject.*tell*()

Example 5.2:

```
fp=open('d:\sample.txt', 'r')
print("Read 10 bytes:",fp.read(10))
print("Current Position:",fp.tell())
```

Output

```
Read 10 bytes: Welcome to
Current Position: 10
```

b) *seek*() method is used to change the current file position.

Syntax:

Fileobject.*seek*(offset[,from])

Where, 'offset' is used to specify how many bytes the pointer is to move. 'from' is an optional argument that specifies the reference position from which position the pointer is to move. 'from' argument takes the following reference positions:

0 – beginning of the file
1 – current position of the file
2 – end of the file

Example 5.3:

```
fp=open('d:\sample.txt', 'r')
print("Read 10 bytes:",fp.read(10))
print("After reading 10 bytes, the current position:",fp.tell())
fp.seek(3,0)#reference position - starting of the file
print("After seek(3,0), the current position:",fp.tell())
print("Read 4 bytes:",fp.read(4))
```

```
fp.seek(0,1)#reference position is current position of the file pointer
print(fp.read())
fp.close()
```

Output

```
Read 10 bytes: Welcome to
After reading 10 bytes, the current position: 10
After seek(3,0), the current position: 3
Read 4 bytes: come
 to Python Programming
```

3. readline()

readline() method is used to read a single line from the input file. This method does not take any argument.

Syntax:

fileobject.*readline*()

Example 5.4:

```
fp=open('d:\pythonintro.txt', 'r')
#The file contains two lines; 'Welcome to Python Programming' &
#'Python is a general-purpose language'
print(fp.readline())
fp.seek(0,1)
print(fp.readline())
fp.close()
```

Output

```
Welcome to Python Programming
Python is a general-purpose language.
```

4. readlines()

readlines() method is used to read all lines from the input file. This method doesn't take any argument.

Syntax:

fileobject.*readlines*()

Example 5.5:

```
fp=open('d:\pythonintro.txt', 'r')
print(fp.readlines())
fp.close()
```

Output

```
['Welcome to Python Programming\n', 'Python is a general-purpose language. \n', 'It has wide range of applications from Web development, scientific and mathematical computing to desktop graphical user Interfaces. ']
```

5. File Object Attributes

The following attributes are used in file object:

file.closed - Returns *True* if file is closed, *False* otherwise.

file.mode - Returns the mode of operation which was used in *open*

file.name - Returns the name of the file.

Example 5.6

```
fp=open('d:\pythonintro.txt', 'r')
print(fp.name)
print(fp.closed)
print(fp.mode)
```

Output:

```
d:\pythonintro.txt
False
r
```

6. Handle

Handle is used to manipulate the file. If the file *open* function is successfully completed, then the Operating System returns a file handle.

File handle is not the content of the file but it is a 'handle' used to read the content of the file.

Example 5.7:

```
fp=open('d:\sample.txt','r')#fp is the  handle
print(fp)
```

Output:

```
<_io.TextIOWrapper name='d:\\sample.txt' mode='r' encoding='cp1252'>
```

Example 5.8:

```
#Counting lines in a file
fp=open('d:\pythonintro.txt')
#The file contains two lines; 'Welcome to Python Programming' &
#'Python is a general-purpose language'
```

```
count=0
for i in fp:
    count=count+1
print(count)
```

Output:

```
2
```

Example 5.9:

```
#If statement in for loop
fp=open('d:\pythonintro.txt')
for i in fp:
    if i.startswith('Python'):
        print(i)
```

Output:

```
Python is a general-purpose language.
```

5.2.2 Writing a File

For writing the data into a file, first the file is opened in 'w' mode. Then using the file method *write*() or *writelines*() the contents are written into the file. If the file already exists then the existing content is deleted and the file pointer is set to the beginning of the file. If the file does not exist then a new file is created.

a) write() method is used to write a single line into the specified file. This method does not add a newline character ('\n') to the end of the line.

Syntax:

Fileobject.*write*(string)

Where, 'string' is the content to be written into the file.

For Example,

```
>>> fp=open('d:\sample.txt', 'w')
>>> fp.write("Algorithm is a step by step procedure")
37 # no. of characters written into the file
>>> fp.close()
>>> fp=open('d:\sample.txt', 'r')
>>> fp.read()
'Algorithm is a step by step procedure'
```

b) *writelines*() method is used to write multiple lines into the specified file.

Syntax:

fileobject.writelines(string)

Example 5.10:

```
f=open('d:\sample.txt','w')
f.writelines(['Algorithm\n','Flowchart\n','Pseudocode\n'])
f.close()
f=open('d:\sample.txt','r')
print(f.read())
f.close()
```

Output:

```
Algorithm
Flowchart
Pseudocode
```

5.2.3 Closing a File

close() method is used to close the file object. After closing, it is not possible to do any operations on that file object without opening it.

Syntax:

```
fileobject.close()
```

Example 5.11:

```
# Open a file
fp=open('d:\sample.txt', 'w')
print("Name of the file: ", fp.name)
# Close the opened file
fp.close()
print("File closed True/False:",fp.closed)
```

Output

```
Name of the file:  d:\sample.txt
File closed True/False: True
```

5.2.4 Renaming and deleting a file

These file processing operations are available in Python *os* module. Before performing these operations first the os module is imported using *import*.

a) *rename*() method is used to change the name of the file.

Syntax:

```
os.rename("old file name","new file name")
```

Example 5.12:

```
import os
os.rename("d:\sam.txt","d:\pythonintro.txt")
print("File renamed")
fp=open("d:\pythonintro.txt")#default mode is 'r'
print(fp.read())
```

Output

File renamed
Welcome to Python Programming
Python is a general-purpose language.
It has wide range of applications from Web development, scientific and mathematical computing to desktop graphical user Interfaces.

b) *remove*() method is used to delete the existing file.

Syntax:

os.remove (" file name")

Example 5.13:

```
import os
os.remove ("d:\sample.txt")# sample.txt is removed from the specified path
```

5.3 FORMAT OPERATOR

Format operator (%) is an operator that takes a format string and a tuple and generates a string that includes the elements of the tuple which is formatted as specified by the format string.

Format string is a string used with the format operator that contains format sequence.

Format sequence is a sequence of characters in a format string, like %d, that specifies how a value should be formatted.

5.3.1 Basic Formatting

Table 3.3 in Unit III contains the basic format symbols used in print function. Basic formatting using those symbols is used, if the order of the arguments is not likely to change and there are only few elements to concatenate.

For Example,

```
>>> print("%d %s"%(2,"Hello"))
2 Hello
>>> print("%d,%g,%s"%(2,5.0,"Hello"))
2,5,Hello
>>> print("%d,%f,%s"%(2,5.0,"Hello"))
2,5.000000,Hello
>>> print("%e,%d"%(23.56,59))
2.356000e+01,59
```

Curly braces {} are also used for formatting.

For Example,

```
>>> '{}{}'.format('one','two')
'onetwo'
>>> '{} {}'.format('one','two')
'one two'
>>> '{1} {0}'.format('one','two')
'two one'
```

5.3.2 Padding and aligning strings

The value to be printed may be padded with specific length.

```
>>> print("%10s"%("sample"))#Right Alignment
    sample
>>> print("%-10s"%("sample"))#Left Alignment
sample
>>> '{:>10}'.format("sample")#Right Alignment in 10 spaces within quotes
'    sample'
>>> '{:10}'.format("sample")#Left Alignment in 10 spaces within quotes
'sample    '
```

5.3.3 Truncating long strings

Inverse to padding is to truncate overly long values to a specific number of characters.

For Example,

```
>>> "%.5s"%('malayalam')
'malay'
>>> '{:.5}'.format('malayalam') #displays 5 characters from the beginning
'malay'
```

It is possible to combine truncating and padding. For example,

```
>>> "%10.5s"%('malayalam')
'     malay'
>>> '{:10.5}'.format('malayalam')
'malay     '
```

5.3.4 Datetime

{} style formatting allows objects to control their own rendering. This, for example, allows datetime objects to be formatted inline.

```
>>> from datetime import datetime
>>> '{:%Y-%m-%d %H:%M}'.format(datetime(2020,8,15,2,50))
'2020-08-15 02:50'
```

5.4 COMMAND LINE ARGUMENTS

The Python **sys** module provides access to any command-line arguments via the **sys.argv**.

- sys.argv is the list of command-line arguments.
- len(sys.argv) is the number of command-line arguments.

Here sys.argv[0] is the program i.e., script name.

For Example,

```
import sys
print('Number of arguments:', len(sys.argv), 'arguments.')
print('Argument List:', str(sys.argv))
```

The above file is run using shift+F5 and then passing the command line arguments.

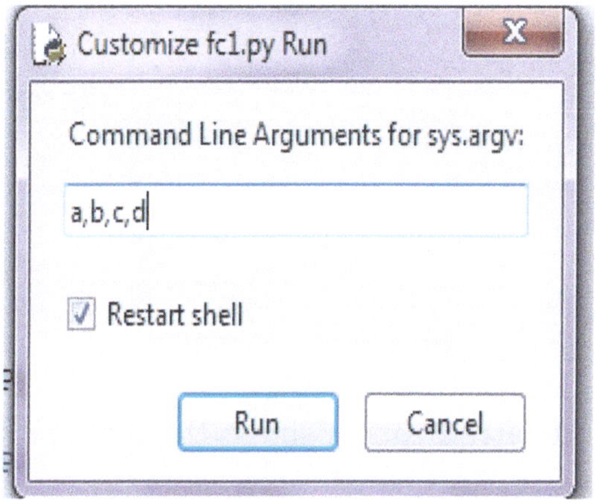

Output:

```
Number of arguments: 2 arguments.
Argument List: ['C:/Users/Arockia Mary/AppData/Local/Programs/Python/Python37-32/fc1.py', 'a,b,c,d']
```

5.5 ERRORS AND EXCEPTIONS

While executing a program, some unexpected conditions may occur that violate some rules of the language. These conditions are referred as errors. If the errors occur due to violation of syntax rules then they will be handled by the compiler. But some errors are not handled by the compiler. Those types of errors abruptly stop the program. These are called as exception. An exception is an event which occurs during the execution of the program that disrupts the normal execution flow of the program. These exceptions are managed by exception handling.

5.5.1 Types of errors:

Errors occur due to incorrect actions. The errors are also called bugs. If the program is bug-free then it provides accurate result. There are three types of errors:

1. Compile time error
2. Logical error
3. Run time error

1. Compile time errors

Compile time errors occur at the time of compilation. These types of errors occur due to violation of syntax rules of the language such as missing of colon (:), missing of bracket, double quotes or incorrect starting of the indentation block and so on. If compilation errors occur then the program will not run until the user corrects them. The following screenshot shows some compile time error. For example, if the colon is missing in *if* condition then it shows syntax error (invalid syntax).

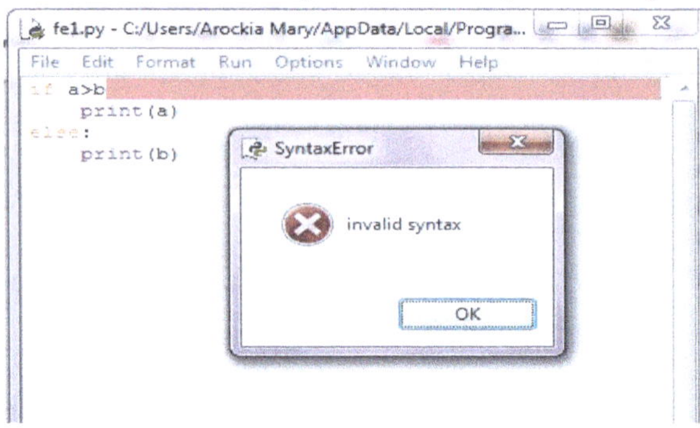

If the indentation is not correct then it shows the syntax error(unexpected indent)

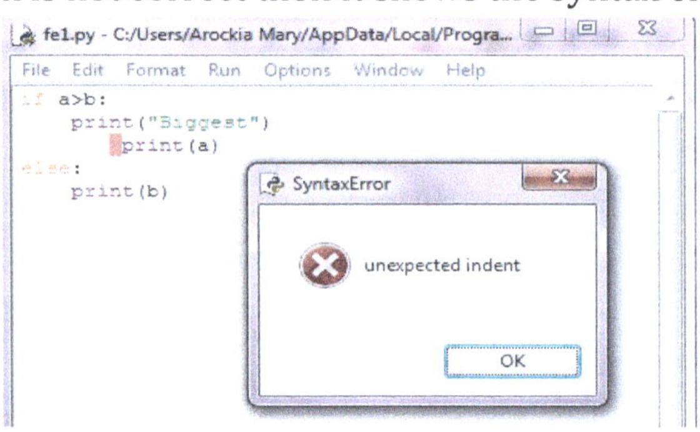

2. Logical error

Logical errors occur due to wrong logic of the program. This type of error neither raises an error at compile time nor abruptly stops the execution of the program. This error always produces the wrong result. The programmer will have to check the logic of the code thoroughly and remove the error.

3. Runtime error

Runtime errors occur during the execution of the program. These errors are not handled by the compiler or interpreter. Runtime errors can stop the execution of the program abruptly. Runtime errors are also called as exception. Examples are Division by zero, and List index out of range. These types of errors are handled by exception handling.

5.5.2 Exception:

An exception is an event that occurs during the execution of the program that stops the normal execution of the program. Therefore, some mechanisms are needed to handle this situation. These mechanisms are called as exception handling. These mechanisms do not halt the program.

All the exceptions in the Python program are represented as classes. There can be some inbuilt exceptions that may contain information about the inaccurate actions that usually occur in the program while running, such as Division by zero, index out of bounds and so on. Exception class is a base class for all the exceptions that can occur in the program.

Types of Exception

There are two types of exceptions that occur in a Python program such as built-in exceptions and user-defined exceptions. Built-in exceptions are known to the Python program and it can be easily handled by creating object of that class. But user-defined exceptions are defined by the user in the program and there is a need to implement the code to define and handle user-defined exceptions.

Few in-built exceptions are:

Exceptions	-	This is the base class for all kinds of exceptions. An object of the Exception class is created to handle any exception that occurs in the program.
Arithmetic Error	-	This is a base class for all arithmetic errors in numeric calculations like Over Flow Error, Floating Point Error, etc.
Over Flow	-	It is raised when calculations exceed the maximum limit for numeric type of operations.
Floating Point Error	-	It is raised when the floating point calculations fail.
Zero Division Error	-	It is raised when some number is divided by zero. It occurs for all numeric type of calculations.
EOF Error	-	It is raised when no input is passed to the input function or the file pointer reaches the end of the file.
Index Error	-	It is raised when the index is not found in the sequence like list, tuple, string and so on.
Syntax Error	-	It is raised when a violation of the syntax rule of the program is found.
Indentation Error	-	It is triggered when indentation of a block is not performed.

5.5.3 Exception Handling

The exception handling is a mechanism that provides the way to handle the exceptions that occur at runtime. The purpose of exception handling is to avoid stopping the program abruptly. For that a piece of code is written to handle that exception and stop the program with some message.

Structure of Exception Handling

Exceptions are handled using three different blocks such as:

1. *try*
2. *except*
3. *finally*

1. The *try* block

A set of statements that may cause errors during the runtime are to be written in the *try* block.

Syntax:

```
try:
        statements
```

The *try* block is written using the keyword *try* and it contains one or multiple statements that may raise errors at runtime.

2. The *except* block

If errors are raised during runtime then the exception details are to be displayed as written in the *except* block. The *except* block is executed only when a certain type of exception occurs in the execution of statements written in the *try* block.

Syntax:

```
except exception_name:
        Statements
```

The *except* block is written for handling a particular type of exception that occurs in the *try* block. For example, except Type Error. This *except* block is used to handle the Type Error exception only.

3. The *finally* block

The *finally* block is the last block written while writing an exception handler in the program. The *finally* block includes a set of statements that need to be executed to perform clean up actions, which closes the file or terminates other processes which are running or closes the connection with the database and so on. It is an optional one. When it is given the *finally* block execute irrespective of whether an exception occurs in the program or not.

Syntax:

```
finally:
        statements
```

Example 5.14: Program to handle ZeroDivisionError

```
try:
    x=int(input("Enter the 1st number: "))
    y=int(input("Enter the 2nd number: "))
    z=x/y
    print("%d/%d = %f"%(x,y,z))
except ZeroDivisionError:
    print("2nd number can not be zero")
finally:
    print("Program Ends")
```

Output:

```
Enter the 1st number: 43
Enter the 2nd number: 0
2nd number can not be zero
Program Ends
```

5.6 MODULES

A module is used to logically organize the Python code. A module is simply a file that defines one or more related functions grouped together. It makes the code easier to understand and use. The functions in a module can be reused by importing the module.

The Python code for a module must be named and stored in memory as filename.py. Here is an example of a simple module called 'display.py'.

```
def print_func(a):
    print("Hi! ",a)
    return
```

5.6.1 The *import* Statement

Any Python source file can act as a module through an *import* statement in some other Python source file.

Syntax:

```
import module1[, module2[,... moduleN]]
```

When the interpreter encounters an *import* statement, it imports the module if the module is present in the search path. A search path is a list of directories that the interpreter searches before importing a module. For example,

```
#import module display
import display
display.print_func("Joash")
```

Output:

Hi! Joash

Python's *import* loads a Python module into its own namespace. Any reference to a name inside the module is made by the module name followed by a dot in front of references to the name.

Example 5.15:

```
#Module - fibonacci.py
def fib(n):   # write Fibonacci series up to n
  a, b = 0, 1
  while a < n:
    print(a, end=' ')
    a, b = b, a+b
  print()
def fib2(n):   # return Fibonacci series up to n
  result = []
  a, b = 0, 1
  while a < n:
    result.append(a)
    a, b = b, a+b
  return result
>>> import Fibonacci
#Using the module name, it is possible to access the function.
>>> fibonacci.fib(500)
0 1 1 2 3 5 8 13 21 34 55 89 144 233 377
>>> fibonacci.fib2(100)
[0, 1, 1, 2, 3, 5, 8, 13, 21, 34, 55, 89]
```

If the function is frequently used then assign it to a local name.

```
>>> fib=fibonacci.fib
>>> fib(500)
0 1 1 2 3 5 8 13 21 34 55 89 144 233 377
```

5.6.2 The *from...import* Statement

Python's *from* statement is used to import the specific names (attributes) from a module into the current namespace.

Syntax:

```
from modulename import name1[, name2[, ... nameN]]
```

For example, to import the function 'square' from the module 'area', use the following statement –

```
from area import square
```

This statement does not import the entire module ***area*** into the current namespace; it just introduces the item ***square*** from the module area into the global symbol table of the importing module.

5.6.3 The *from...import* * Statement

All names from a module can also be imported into the current namespace by using the following import statement –

```
from modulename import *
```

This provides an easy way to import all the items from a module into the current namespace.

For example,

```
#Module area.py
def square(a):
  area=4*a
  print("Area of square = ",area)
  return
```

from loads a Python module into the current namespace, so that it is referred without the need to mention the module name again:

```
from area import square
square(4)
```

Output:

```
Area of square =  16
```

5.6.4 Locating Modules

If a module is imported then the Python interpreter searches for the module in the following sequences –

- The current directory.
- If the module is not found, Python then searches each directory in the shell variable PYTHONPATH.
- If all else fails, Python checks the default path. On UNIX, the default path is normally /usr/local/lib/python/. On Windows the default path is C:\Users\AppData\Local\Programs\Python\Python38

The module search path is stored in the system module *sys* as the *sys.path* variable. The *sys.path* variable contains the current directory, PYTHONPATH, and the installation-dependent default.

5.6.5 The *PYTHONPATH* Variable

The PYTHONPATH is an environment variable, consisting of a list of directories. The syntax of PYTHONPATH is the same as that of the shell variable PATH.

A PYTHONPATH from a Windows system:

set PYTHONPATH = c:\python20\lib;

A PYTHONPATH from a UNIX system:

set PYTHONPATH = /usr/local/lib/python

5.6.6 Namespaces and Scoping

Variables are names (identifiers) that map to objects. A *namespace* is a dictionary of variable names (keys) and their corresponding objects (values).

A Python statement can access variables in a *local namespace* and in the *global namespace*. If a local and a global variable have the same name, the local variable takes precedence over the global variable.

Each function has its own local namespace. Class methods follow the same scoping rule as ordinary functions.

Python assumes that any variable assigned a value in a function is local. Therefore, in order to assign a value to a global variable within a function, the *global* statement must be used.

The statement *global VarName* tells Python that VarName is a global variable. Python stops searching the local namespace for the variable.

For example, a variable ***M*** is defined in the global namespace. Within the function ***M*** is assigned as ***M***+1, therefore Python assumes ***M*** as a local variable. If the local variable M is accessed before setting it, so an UnboundLocalError is the result. Uncommenting the global statement fixes the problem.

```
M = 200
def AddM():
  # Uncomment the following line to fix the code:
  # global Money
  M = M + 1

print(M)
AddM()
print(M)
```

Output:

```
200
Traceback (most recent call last):
  File "C:/Users/Arockia Mary/AppData/Local/Programs/Python/Python37-32/Me1.py", line 8, in <module>
    AddM()
```

```
File "C:/Users/Arockia Mary/AppData/Local/Programs/Python/Python37-32/Me1.py", line 5, in AddM
    M = M + 1
UnboundLocalError: local variable 'M' referenced before assignment
```

datetime module

datetime module is used to get the current date and time of the local system.

For example,

```
#date.py
from datetime import datetime
print(datetime.now())
```

Output:

```
2020-08-10 17:53:04.103997
```

5.7 PACKAGES

A package is a hierarchical file directory structure that defines a single Python application environment that consists of modules and subpackages and sub-subpackages, and so on.

A directory must contain a file named __init__.py to consider it as a package. It is an empty file.

Two ways of importing sub-module are

1. import pack.start.sum
2. from pack.start import sum

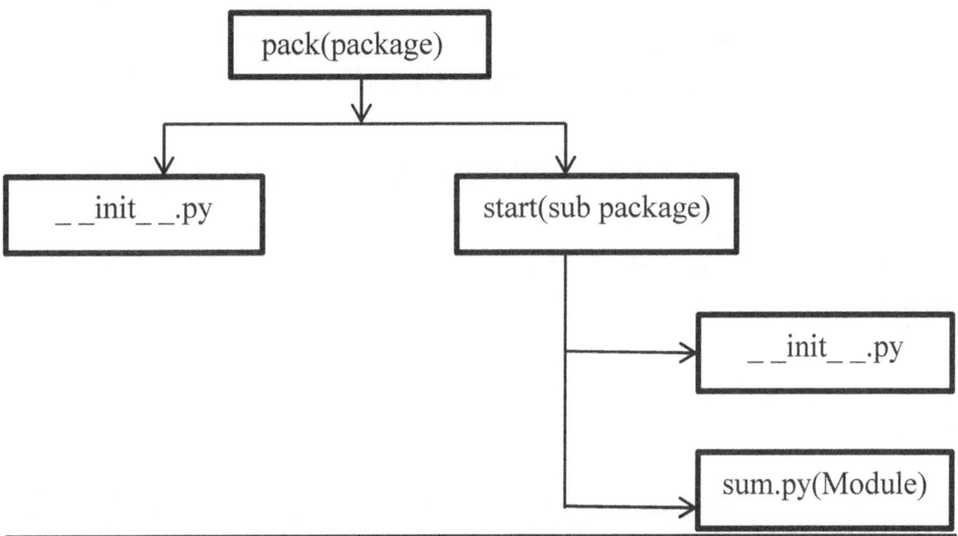

Example 5.16:

```
#sum.py
def add(a,b):
  return a*b
#file.py
import pack.start.sum # user-defined package
print(pack.start.sum.add(5,10))
```

Output:

```
50
```

5.8 ILLUSTRATIVE PROGRAMS

5.8.1 Word Count

Write a Python program to count the number of words in the file: d:\\source.txt which contains the following sentences.

"Welcome to Python Programming.
Python is a powerful high-level, object-oriented programming language.
Python has simple easy-to-use syntax."

Program:

```
filename=input("Enter the file name: ")
fp=open(filename,"r")
wc=fp.read().split()
print("Number of words in the file: ",filename,len(wc))
fp.close()
```

Output:

```
Enter the file name: d:\\source.txt
Number of words in the file:  d:\\source.txt 17
```

5.8.2 Write a Python program to count the frequency of words without Module

Program:

```
filename=input("Enter the file name: ")
fp=open(filename,"r")
d=dict()
wc=fp.read().split()
for w in wc:
  if w in d:
    d[w]+=1
  else:
```

```
        d[w]=1
    print(d)
    fp.close()
```

Output:

```
Enter the file name: d:\\source.txt
{'Welcome': 1, 'to': 1, 'Python': 3, 'Programming.': 1, 'is': 1, 'a': 1, 'powerful': 1, 'high-level,': 1, 'object-oriented': 1, 'programming': 1, 'language': 1, 'has': 1, 'simple': 1, 'easy-to-use': 1, 'syntax.': 1}
```

5.8.3 Write a Python program to count the frequency of words with the predefined module *collections*

Program:

```
from collections import Counter
filename=input("Enter the file name: ")
fp=open(filename,"r")
print("Number of words in the file ",filename)
print(Counter(fp.read().split()))
fp.close()
```

Output:

```
Enter the file name: d:\\source.txt
Number of words in the file  d:\\source.txt
Counter({'Python': 3, 'Welcome': 1, 'to': 1, 'Programming.': 1, 'is': 1, 'a': 1, 'powerful': 1, 'high-level,': 1, 'object-oriented': 1, 'programming': 1, 'language': 1, 'has': 1, 'simple': 1, 'easy-to-use': 1, 'syntax.': 1})
```

5.8.4 Copy a File

Write a Python program to copy the source file d:\\source.txt into destination file d:\\dest.txt.

d:\\source.txt contains the following sentences:

"Welcome to Python Programming.

Python is a powerful high-level, object-oriented programming language.

Python has simple easy-to-use syntax."

Program 1.: #Using the predefined module shutil

```
from shutil import copyfile
source=input("Enter the source file name: ")
dest=input("Enter the destination file name: ")
copyfile(source,dest)
```

```
print("File copied successfully")
print("Contents of the destination file:")
fp=open(dest,"r")
print(fp.read())
```

Output:

```
Enter the source file name: d:\\source.txt
Enter the destination file name: d:\\dest.txt
File copied successfully
Contents of the destination file:
Welcome to Python Programming.
Python is a powerful high-level, object-oriented programming language.
Python has simple easy-to-use syntax.
```

Program 2.:#Without Module

```
source=input("Enter the source file name: ")
dest=input("Enter the destination file name: ")
fps=open(source,"r")
contents=fps.read()
fpd=open(dest,"w")
fpd.write(contents)
fps.close()
fpd.close()
print("File copied successfully")
print("Contents of the destination file:")
fp=open(dest,"r")
print(fp.read())
fp.close()
```

Output:

```
Enter the source file name: d:\\source.txt
Enter the destination file name: d:\\dest1.txt
File copied successfully
Contents of the destination file:
Welcome to Python Programming.
Python is a powerful high-level, object-oriented programming language.
Python has simple easy-to-use syntax.
```

Short Questions

1. What is a text file?

Text file is formed with a sequence of lines. Each line includes a sequence of words. Each word has a sequence of characters. Each line is terminated with a special character, called EOL (End Of Line) character.

2. Write a python program that writes "Hello world" into a file.

```
fp =open("sample.txt",'w')
fp.write("Hello world")
fp.close()
```

3. Write a python program that counts the number of words in a file.

```
filename=input("Enter the file name: ")
fp=open(filename,"r")
wc=fp.read().split()
print("Number of words in the file: ",filename,len(wc))
fp.close()
```

4. What are the two arguments taken by the open() function?

The open function takes two arguments:

1. name of the file and
2. the mode of operation.

Example: f = open("test.dat","w")

Where "test.dat" is the name of the file and "w" is the mode of operation.

5. What is a file object?

A file object allows the user to use, access and manipulate all the user-accessible files. It maintains the state about the file it has opened.

6. What information is displayed if we print a file object in the given program?

```
f= open("test.txt","w")
print (f)
```

The name of the file, mode and the encoding details will be displayed.

Output: <_io.TextIOWrapper name='test.txt' mode='w' encoding='cp1252'>

7. What is an exception?

An exception is an event that occurs during the execution of the program that stops the normal execution of the program.

8. What are the error messages that are displayed for the following exceptions?

a. Accessing a non-existent list item
b. Accessing a key that is not in the dictionary
c. Trying to open a non-existent file

a. IndexError: list index out of range
b. KeyError: name of the key
c. IOError: [Errno 2] No such file or directory: 'filename'

9. What are the two parts in an error message?

The error message has two parts:

1. the type of error before the colon and
2. details about the error after the colon.

Example:
IndexError: list index out of range
KeyError: name of the key

10. How do you handle the exception inside a program when you try to open a non-existent file?

'try' block may be used as below:

```
filename = input('Enter a file name: ')
try:
    f = open (filename, "r")
except IOError:
    print( 'There is no file named', filename)
```

11. How does *try* and *except* work?

- A set of statements that may cause errors during the runtime are to be written in the *try* block.
- If the errors are raised during runtime then the exception details are to be displayed as written in the *except* block. The *except* block is executed only when a certain type of exception occurs in the execution of statements written in the *try* block.
- The *except* block is written for handling a particular type of exception that occurs in the *try* block. For example, except TypeError. This *except* block is used to handle the TypeError exception only.

12. What is the function of *raise* statement? What are its two arguments?

The *raise* statement is used to raise an exception when the program detects an error. It takes two arguments: the exception type and specific information about the error.

Example:

```
x='hi'
if not type(x) is int:
    raise TypeError("Only integers are allowed")
```

13. What is the use of the format operator?

- Format operator (%) is an operator that takes a format string and a tuple and generates a string that includes the elements of the tuple which is formatted as specified by the format string.
- Format string is a string used with the format operator that contains format sequence.
- Format sequence is a sequence of characters in a format string, like %d that specifies how a value should be formatted.

14. What are modules?

A module is used to logically organize the Python code. A module is simply a file that defines one or more related functions grouped together. It makes the code easier to understand and use. The functions in a module can be reused by importing the module.

15. What is a package?

Packages are namespaces that may contain multiple packages and modules themselves. They are simply directories.

Syntax: from <mypackage> import <modulename>

16. What is the special file that each package in Python must contain?

Each package in Python must contain a special file called _init_.py

17. How do you delete a file in Python?

The remove() method is used to delete a file by supplying the name of the file to be deleted as argument.

Syntax: os.remove(filename)

18. How do you use command line arguments to give input to the program?

The Python **sys** module provides access to any command-line arguments via the **sys.argv**.

- *sys.argv* is the list of command-line arguments.
- len(sys.argv) is the number of command-line arguments.

Here *sys.argv[0]* is the program i.e., script name.

Unsolved Exercises

1. Write a Python program to read first n lines of a file.
2. Write a Python program to read last n lines of a file.
3. Write a Python program to append text to a file and display the text.
4. Write a Python program to read a file line by line and store it into a list.
5. Write a Python program to find the longest words.
6. Write a Python program to count the number of lines in a text file.

7. Write a Python program to combine each line from first file with the corresponding line in second file.
8. Write a Python program to assess if a file is closed or not.
9. In a large collection of MP3 files, there may be more than one copy of the same song stored in different directories or with different file names. The goal of this exercise is to search for these duplicates.
   1. Write a program that searches a directory and all of its subdirectories, recursively, and returns a list of complete paths for all files with a given suffix(like .mp3). Hint: os.path provides several useful functions for manipulating file and path names.
   2. To recognize duplicates, you can use a hash function that reads the files and generates a short summary of the contents. For example, MD5 takes an arbitrary-long 'message' and returns a 128-bit 'checksum'. The probability is very small that two files with different contents will return the same checksum.

B.E./B.Tech DEGREE EXAMINATION, JANUARY 2018
First Semester
PROBLEM SOLVING AND PYTHON PROGRAMMING
(Common to All Branches)
(Regulation 2017)

Time : Three Hours **Maximum : 100**

Marks
Answer ALL questions

PART A

(10X2=20 Marks)

1. What is an algorithm?
2. Write an algorithm to accept two numbers, compute the sum and print the result.
3. Name the four types of scalar objects Python has.
4. What is a tuple? How literals of type tuple are written? Give example.
5. Write a Python program to accept two numbers, multiply them and print the result.
6. Write a Python program to accept two numbers, find the greatest and print the result.
7. What is a list? How lists differ from tuples?
8. How to slice a list in Python?
9. Write a Python script to display the current date and time.
10. Write a note on modular design.

PART B

(5X16=80 Marks)

11. a) i) Draw a flow chart to accept three distinct numbers, find the greatest and print the result. (8)

ii) Draw a flow chart to find the sum of the series 1+2+3+4+5+...+100 (8)

(OR)

b) Outline the Towers of Hanoi problem. Suggest a solution to the Towers of Hanoi problem with relevant diagrams. (16)

12. a) i) What is a numeric literal? Give Examples. (4)

ii) Appraise the arithmetic operators in Python with an example. (12)

(OR)

b) i) Outline the operator precedence of arithmetic operators in Python. (6)

ii) Write a Python program to exchange the value of two variables. (4)

iii) Write a Python program using function to find the sum of first 'n' even numbers and print the result. (6)

13. a) i) Appraise with an example nested if and elif header in Python. (6)

ii) Explain with an example while loop, break statement and continue statement in Python. (10)

(OR)

b) i) Write a Python program to find the factorial of a given number without recursion and with recursion. (8)

ii) Write a Python program to generate first 'N' Fibonacci numbers. (8)

Note : The Fibonacci numbers are 0,1,1,2,3,5,8,13,21,34,....where each number is the sum of the preceding two.

14. a) i) What is a dictionary in Python? Give example. (4)

ii) Appraise the operations for dynamically manipulating dictionaries. (12)

(OR)

b) i) Write a Python program to perform linear search on a list. (8)

ii) Write a python program to store 'n' numbers in a list and sort the list using selection sort. (8)

15. a) Tabulate the different modes for opening a file and explain the same. (16)

(OR)

b) i) Appraise the use of try block and except block in Python with syntax. (6)

ii) Explain with an example exceptions with arguments in Python. (10)

B.E./B.Tech DEGREE EXAMINATION, APRIL/MAY 2019

First Semester

PROBLEM SOLVING AND PYTHON PROGRAMMING

(Common to All Branches)

(Regulation 2017)

Time : Three Hours **Maximum : 100 Marks**

Answer ALL questions

PART A (10x2=20 Marks)

1. List the symbols used in drawing the flowchart.(Ref. Page no. 1.11)
2. Give the Python code to find the minimum among the list of 10 numbers.
3. Outline the logic to swap the contents of two identifiers without using third variable.
4. State about Logical operators available in python language with example.
5. Comment with an example on the use of local and global variable with the same identifier name.
6. Define recursive function.
7. How to create a list in python? Illustrate the use of negative indexing of list with example.
8. Demonstrate with simple code to draw the histogram in python.
9. Categorize the different types of errors that arise during programming. Interpret the following python code

```
>>> import os
>>> cwd = os.getcwd( )
>>> print cwd
/home/dinsdale
```

10. What is command line argument?

PART B

(5x16=80 Marks)

11. a) Mention the different types of iterative structure allowed in Python. Explain the use of continue and break statements with an example. (16)

(OR)

b) i) What is an algorithm ? Summarize the characteristics of a good algorithm. (8)

ii) Outline the algorithm for displaying the first n odd numbers. (8)

12. a) Describe about the concept of precedence and associativity of operators with example. (16)

(OR)

b) i) Mention the list of keywords available in Python. Compare it with variable name. (8)

ii) What are statements? How are they constructed from variable and expression in Python? (8)

13. a) i) Analyze string slicing. Illustrate how it is done in Python with example. (8)

ii) Write a Python code to search a string in a given list. (8)

(OR)

b) i) Outline about function definition and call with example. (10)

ii) Why are functions needed? (6)

14. a) Demonstrate with code the various operations that can be performed on tuples. (16)

(OR)

b) Outline the algorithm and write a Python program to sort the numbers in ascending order using merge sort. (16)

15. a) Explain about the file reading and writing operation using format operator with Python code. (16)

(OR)

b) i) Explain about how exception are handled with examples. (8)

ii) Design a Python code to count the number of words in a Python file. (8)

B.E./B.Tech. DEGREE EXAMINATION, DECEMBER/JANUARY 2019

First Semester

PROBLEM SOLVING AND PYTHON PROGRAMMING

(Common to All Branches)

(Regulation 2017)

Time : Three Hours **Maximum : 100 Marks**

Answer ALL questions

PART A

(10x2=20 Marks)

1. Distinguish between algorithm and program.
2. Write an algorithm to find the minimum number in a given list of numbers.
3. What are keywords? Give example.
4. State the reasons to divide programs into functions.
5. Present the flow of execution for a while statement.
6. Define recursion with an example.
7. Relate strings and lists.
8. Give a function that can take a value and return the first key mapping to that value in a dictionary.
9. What is a module? Give example.
10. Find the syntax error in the code given:
    while True print('Hello world')

PART B

(5x16=80 Marks)

11. a) i) Discuss about the building blocks of algorithms. (8)

    ii) Write a recursive algorithm to solve towers of Hanoi problem. (8)

    (OR)

    b) i) Identify the simple strategies for developing an algorithm. (8)

    ii) Write an algorithm to insert a card into a list of sorted cards. (8)

12. a) i) Sketch the structures of interpreter and compiler. Detail the differences between them. Explain how python works in interactive mode and script mode with examples. (2+2+4)

    ii) Summarize the precedence of mathematical operators in python. (8)

    (OR)

b) i) Explain the syntax and structure of user defined functions in python with examples. Also discuss about parameter passing in function. (12)

ii) Write a Python function to swap the values of two variables. (4)

13.a) List the three types of conditional statements and explain them. (16)

(OR)

b) i) Python strings are immutable. Justify with an example. (8)

ii) Write a Python code to perform binary search. Trace it with an example of your choice. (8)

14.a) i) Discuss the different options to traverse a list. (8)

ii) Demonstrate the working of + ,* and slice operators in python. (8)

(OR)

b) i) Compare and contrast tuples and lists in pythons. (4)

ii) Write a script in python to sort n numbers using selection sort. (12)

15.a) i) Explain the commands used to read and write into a file with examples. (8)

ii) Discuss about the use of format operator in file processing. (8)

(OR)

b) i) Describe how exceptions are handled in Python with necessary examples. (16)